Emerging from the Crucible

Enduring the Refiner's Fire

Wanda Strange

Property of:
Mary Bailey
Please read and be encouraged.
Wanda is my niece.

Scripture references taken from the King James Version of the Bible

Scripture taken from the HOLY BIBLE, NEW INTERNATIONAL VERSION Copyright 1973, 1978, 1984, by International Bible Society. Used by permission of Zondervan. All Rights reserved.

Scripture taken from *The Message*. Copyright © 1993, 1994, 1995, 1996, 2000, 2001, 2002. Used by permission of NavPress Publishing Group

Copyright © 2018 Wanda Strange

Publisher: bylisabell
Radical Women
(DBA)
PO Box 782
Granbury, TX
76048
www.bylisabell.com

All rights reserved.
ISBN-10: **1-7325363-0-9**
ISBN-13: **978-1-7325363-0-2**

DEDICATION

*I lovingly dedicate
Emerging from the Crucible
to
my daughter, Ginger,
and my husband, Kerry*

Table of Contents

Hidden Treasure... 6

Chapter 1 Preparing for the Worst.. 9

Chapter 2 What Next.. 17

Chapter 3 Alone in the Storm... 27

Chapter 4 Just When You Thought It Couldn't Get Worse 32

Chapter 5 The Treatment Plan... 39

Chapter 6 Home at Last.. 44

Chapter 7 Are We Done Yet?.. 53

Chapter 8 Who Knew Shingles Caused Worse Pain than Cancer?........... 60

Chapter 9 The Most Memorable Holiday Christmas 1984...................... 63

Chapter 10 The New Normal 67

Chapter 11 Aftereffects 77

Chapter 12 Emotional and Social Issues 88

Chapter 13 Celebrating Life.. 92

Chapter 14 Post Cancer Changing Perspectives 102

Chapter 15 The Future Versus Living in the Moment............................. 116

Chapter 16 Lessons from the Cancer Experience..................................... 120

Chapter 17 Glorifying God Throughout the Fire Storm 135

Chapter 18 What Can I Do? How Can I Help?.. 144

Chapter 19 The Refiner's Purpose 159

Chapter 20 Hanging onto Hope Comforting Scriptures 162

References 171

ABOUT THE AUTHOR 172

ACKNOWLEDGMENTS

I gratefully acknowledge the amazing prayer warriors, who prayed for us through crises and through the telling and retelling of our story

Fellow survivors and strugglers who shared their own experiences

Patients and caregivers who inspired me and taught me to celebrate life

Beta readers who identified and corrected errors in the manuscript

Cheryl Barron for her graphic design expertise

Kelli Ugarte Photography for back cover photo

My sister, Lisa Bell, for her continued encouragement and patience with my technology challenged efforts

Members of Granbury, TX. Living Waters – Roaring Writer's Critique Group for your encouragement and insights

My family for their patient and loving support

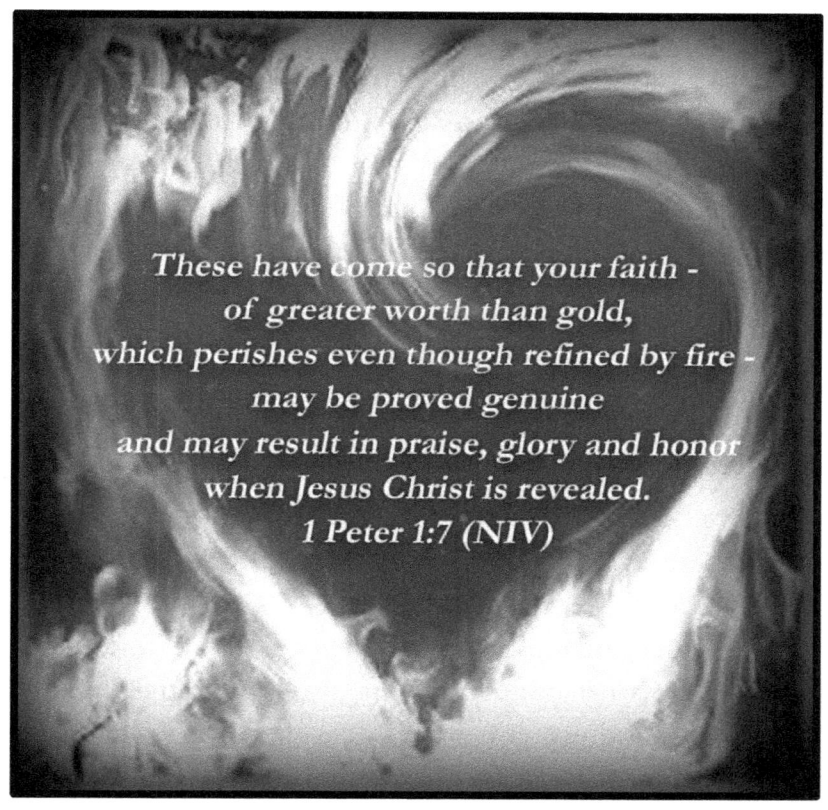

Foreword
Dan L. Griffin

When you add God to the instinctive life force of a ten-year-old, blue-eyed blonde angel, you have a miracle-making formula! Put in her corner two devoted, stop-at-nothing parents, and you will see mountains move!

Ginger Strange had all this going for her when the doctors told her she had a malignant brain tumor. But having strong support and faith gets you only to the beginning of the struggle. This story will grip your soul. As their pastor, I lived through much of it with this amazingly tightknit family. I knew the parameters of their marathon of hospitals, surgeries and recovery, and still my eyes went moist in nearly every chapter.

When medical authorities lay the "C" word on you, every cell in your body tightens. Ginger's little-girl faith buoyed her parents' confidence. The fact that Ginger's mom is a registered nurse only intensified her anxiety, because she knew what they were dealing with.

This breakthrough tale of victory through faith and effort will encourage anyone in a similar situation. Wanda, story weaver and eyewitness of the drama, describes for the reader the often-unexplained facets of how one resumes a life put on hold. We empathize, thanks to Wanda, with Ginger's reaction to the gawking stares of the discourteous when one is permanently bald as a teenager.

Emerging from the Crucible is more than a heart-squeezing look at a child facing a bully of a disease. It is a diary of a mother's worst fears, a no-holds-barred triptych of tough love, nothing less than a manual of how to face the unthinkable without blinking. It is a feast of survival for those hungry for hope.

On nearly every page, the author credits the part played by her tenacious faith that God was not going to let her daughter die. It is full of weeping, laughter, suffering, celebrations, and family unity. Every parent of children, sick or well, should absorb this story until it is a part of them.

Dr. Dan Griffin hails from Oklahoma but has lived in Texas most of his life. In his pastoral career, he has led churches of all sizes. He and Marilyn, his wife of 53 years, have three grown children and five grandchildren. The Griffins live in Arlington, TX. In addition to pastoring, he teaches Bible at Dallas Baptist University as an adjunct professor. He currently serves as pastor of First Baptist Lancaster, 2013 – present. Dan received his BA in English at Oklahoma Baptist University. He continued education at Southern Baptist Theological Seminary in KY, where he received his M. Div. and his D. Min. He received honorary degrees from Campbell University (NC) and Dallas Baptist University.

Preface

From ancient times artisans used gold to produce objects of beauty and worth. The ancients adorned themselves and their homes with precious metals designed by skilled craftsmen. Since early times gold and silver served as mediums of monetary exchange among the nations of the world.

The modern world recognizes silver and gold for many uses beyond value as a monetary standard. In addition to being the source for jewelry and objects of art, they provide resources in electronic applications, the aircraft-aerospace industry, as well as medical, dental and chemical fields.

However, found in their raw form, these metals are neither beautiful nor useful. Before they can be fashioned into objects, the precious metals must be mined, broken, molten, and purged of impurities. The refining and the shaping processes require intense heat and pressure.

The dictionary defines a crucible as a container of metal or refractory material employed for heating substances to high temperature.

A severe test or trial causing lasting change or influence denotes the spiritual or emotional definition of a crucible.

No one in their right mind signs up for purification in the refiner's fire. We may pray with the Psalmist, *Search me...Test me...See if there is any offensive way in me. Psalm 139:23-24, (NIV)* not realizing the testing of our faith comes from suffering. Because we live in a fallen world, we will experience trials. Christ told us *in this world we will have trouble. John 16: 33 (NIV)*

Adversity – suffering – trials – these light the refining fires of our faith. As we endure and persevere through the refining process, God molds us into something of beauty, something useful, something which reflects His glory.

Emerging from the Crucible shares an evolving story of God's refining work in the furnace of adversity. Our family story celebrates God's sustaining grace. Unlike the refining of precious metals, God's refining work is ongoing. He continues to work in all of us, His children, shaping our lives for use in His service. I pray our family's story uplifts, strengthens, and encourages as we celebrate hope and God's miraculous, sustaining power.

Hidden Treasure

Deep within the mountain, one slender vein of undiscovered ore snuggled contentedly in the crevice of a large rock. The huge stones surrounding her home offered a false sense of security. She focused gratefully on the good things of her life. *I'm blessed with so much. I have all I need and much of what I want. I'm comfortable in this safe protected place. I'm tough and strong. Nothing can touch me.*

Suddenly, without warning, an explosion shattered the surrounding rocks, destroying her fortress. Stunned by the violent impact, the solitary element braced for the next assault. Some unseen enemy detonated charges setting off a series of blasts, which followed in quick secession. Unprotected by surrounding rock, the crash ripped her from the security of her hiding place and sent her tumbling down the mountain.

Swept up in an avalanche of rocks, she picked up speed and crashed against the other stones. She tried in vain to regain her footing. An unidentified force propelled her to a seemingly endless descent and controlled each movement. The individual rocks moved as a single mass plummeting to an unknown destination.

At last, the fragmented stones abruptly crashed into a large container. Before the ore gathered her wits, a machine applied intense pressure crushing her along with the surrounding rocks. Her entire being tightened in an attempt to endure the tearing sensation. The last piece of surrounding stone fragmented, separating her from anything familiar.

She relaxed as water filled the tank and a soothing bath washed away the dirt and debris. Much too soon, a brusque splash of liquid fire interrupted the short-lived respite. Swirling acid burned and penetrated to her core. Impurities detached and tore from the precious metal. The ore braced for another attack. *Can this get any worse?*

Beyond her vision, another strange worker pulled the plug allowing liquid to drain and with it the scum. A shovel scooped up the unrefined gold and dumped it onto a conveyer belt. *Oh, no! I'm moving again – intense heat – I can't bear it! Please – STOP! NO!*

Inside the crucible, the melting process began. As the heat grew hotter and hotter, the ore melted. The refiner skimmed slag from the surface of the molten metal. Still impurities remained. So, the molten metal returned to the crucible and submitted again to the intense heat. Again, dross rose to the surface to be removed. The process repeated until at last, the refiner certified the gold as pure.

The molten metal bears no resemblance to the slender vein hidden in the crevice of the rock. The purified gold emerges from the crucible – ready to be molded into something of beauty – something that can be used.

The refiner declares, "Now, she is ready to become all she was created to be."

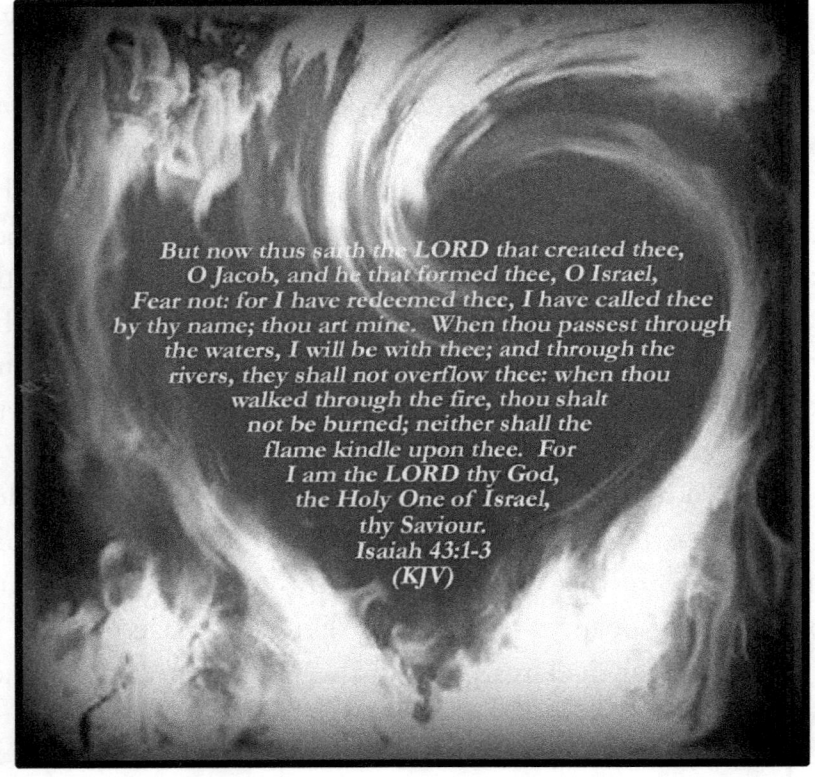

Chapter 1
Preparing for the Worst
Get Ready, The Storm's Coming

August 22, 1984, 2:00 a.m.

I sat alone in the darkened room. A single lamp provided the only illumination in the entire house. Nursing textbooks lay abandoned on the floor beside my chair. The printed words held clinical descriptions of classic symptoms – signs I recognized in my ten-year-old daughter. Everything I read confirmed a devastating condition.

Still, I prayed. *Let me be wrong. This could not be happening – not to Ginger – not to our family.*

Sleep eluded me. *I have to get up in a few hours and hide this terror. I will drive Ginger and her friends to school as if nothing is wrong.*

For weeks we looked forward to the first day of middle school and planned every detail. She begged her daddy for the perfect outfit – a stylish, overpriced jumpsuit – with shoes to match. He acquiesced and paid for her new look. She sported a new, much shorter hairstyle. Before bedtime, she carefully laid out everything she needed for a new beginning.

The summer flew by in a whirlwind of activity. The pace of the season seemed normal for our lives. Ginger attended a flurry of church activities including summer camp at Mount Lebanon in Cedar Hill, TX. I managed to arrange carpools and play dates so she could participate in every possible event.

New Orleans hosted the 1984 World's Fair. We spent months excitedly investigating the details and potential educational opportunities of a driving trip. In early August, we traveled with a neighbor family to see everything possible between Dallas and New Orleans. Unfortunately, Ginger and I saw nothing of the World's Fair except the infirmary. The doctor at the fair diagnosed her with a stomach virus.

I suspected something was wrong with my daughter, though I never imagined it might be serious. All summer Ginger experienced episodes of headaches and vomiting. After a day of sickness, she recovered and seemed her perky self. I took her to the doctor three times that summer. Her pediatrician thought stress might be playing a role. My grandmother died in June. Was it possible she picked up on my sadness, perhaps taking clues from my depression? The transition to middle school caused some anxiety. Could that really be causing all the symptoms?

Up until this August Sunday afternoon, I bought those explanations. As I sat in her bedroom with her friends talking about their plans for the first day of school, Ginger looked across the room at me. I noticed, her eyes crossed. The fancy medical term is *strabismus*. The girls left, and Ginger made her final preparations for the next morning. After my husband and daughter slept soundly, I pulled down the nursing textbooks and saw the words making sleep impossible. "BRAIN TUMOR" Terrorizing thoughts fired in rapid succession. *That's not possible. There has to be another explanation. I am a nurse, not a doctor. What do I know? Surely this can't be.*

Still, somewhere deep inside, I knew something was terribly wrong.

The nursing books held cold, hard facts. In the darkness of that morning, I required more than facts. The biggest challenge of our lives and of my faith loomed.

Though as a very young child I accepted Jesus as my Savior, I lacked spiritual maturity. I trusted and leaned on my personal relationship with Him, but I never faced this kind of test. I understood God provided my strength, but I instinctively knew this challenge required more strength than I possessed. No nursing book could heal the pain or ease the anxiety I felt. I abandoned the textbooks and deferred to the book I trusted for every situation. I reached for my Bible. As I prayed for God's guidance to direct me to the exact words I needed, I let it fall open. It fell to a passage that became my prayer.

As I earnestly prayed these words, I felt a sense of God's presence, peace, and love. There was no promise everything would be okay. I would soon have my worst fears confirmed.

> Create in me a pure heart, O God,
> and renew a steadfast spirit within me.
> Do not cast me from your presence
> or take your Holy Spirit from me.
> Restore to me the joy of your salvation
> and grant me a willing spirit,
> to sustain me.
> Psalm 51:10-12 (NIV)

There was no promise things would be easy. We faced the most difficult time of our lives. God promised to sustain us and uphold us. He promised to be present through each decision and every circumstance we faced.

With this assurance I closed my eyes, still praying for a miracle and slept until we faced the next day's events.

August 23, 1984

The morning started as planned. I dropped the girls off at school. Before leaving home Kerry and I discussed Ginger's health. I shared my suspicion of a serious problem, though not the depths of my fears. I hoped for a simple explanation, something with an easy solution. *No reason to alarm him needlessly.*

My nursing position afforded me the resource of one of the best diagnosticians in Dallas. As soon as I arrived at the office I shared my observations with my employer, who arranged an urgent appointment with an ophthalmologist in our building. I appreciated the definite advantage of knowing how to manipulate the healthcare system.

Somehow I succeeded in the struggle to maintain control of my emotions throughout the workday. At the end of the school day, I picked Ginger up. As we drove to the medical center, she chattered about every detail of her day. She excitedly described her classes, reconnection with friends, and the oddities and niceties of each teacher. Her anxiety about middle school disappeared, as she embraced the challenge of the new year.

When we arrived at the office my boss examined her and confirmed the need for further evaluation. Exhausted, she slept in the exam room until our ophthalmology appointment time. After a brief examination, the doctor turned to me, "Mom, this isn't right."

No kidding. Tell me something I don't know.

The medical confirmation served to escalate my fears. While the staff scheduled an emergent CT scan of Ginger's brain, I called Kerry and asked him to meet us at Baylor University Medical Center.

We waited for what seemed an eternity. Ginger, a typical ten-year-old, grew restless. She explored the halls, roamed into the restricted area, and eavesdropped outside the radiology area. The familiar voice of her trusted friend laughed and joked with another physician.

Later, she recalled what seemed a painful betrayal. "I knew everything was okay. I heard D---- laughing and joking with the other doctors. How could he do that when I was so sick?"

This experience provided a life lesson which remained with me throughout my career. How often I inadvertently behaved similarly, laughing and joking at the moment someone in a nearby room received devastating news. Humor provides essential stress relief for professional caregivers. However, every physician and nurse should be careful where, when, and how a moment of levity is perceived, being aware of the feelings of patients and family members who overhear conversations.

I worked with these physicians daily, knew them well and trusted their judgment. They carefully reviewed and discussed the scans. Perhaps they delayed sharing the report and with it, an inevitable crisis. They knew and loved Ginger. Not known as a center for pediatric services, Baylor cares for very few children. They saw her because of our working relationship and none of them wanted to say the words which would devastate our world. No doctor wants to deliver bad news any more than the patient and family wants to hear it.

Finally, the doctor emerged from the reading room. He sat down and spoke as gently as possible. "There is no easy way to say this. The scan reveals a mass at the base of Ginger's brain. We need to move quickly. She needs immediate intervention."

Two words – *brain tumor* – changed our lives forever.

Initially, shock allowed us to rationally listen to the physician as he described the details of the scan results and explained the next steps. As he stood and exited the waiting room, the medical personnel scurried behind him to make the arrangements for transfer of Ginger's care to Children's Medical Center. The necessary phone calls afforded the staff an escape from the palpable pain filling the room.

Left alone in the waiting room, the three of us clung to each other and wept. We struggled to absorb the information and process a flood of emotions; disbelief – confusion – numbness – terror – at a loss for what to do next.

As shock gave way to fear and desperation, I suppressed the urge to scream. *I have to be strong for my baby and for my husband. If I succumb to this fear, the resulting hysteria will render me incompetent. They need me to hold it together.*

I held my little girl while we both cried. I desperately wanted to make everything okay. *I'm her mother – I need to fix this. But this isn't fixable with my limited skills.*

Ginger exhibited the first of many protective coping mechanisms. Denial surfaced and her rationale made perfect sense. She stated as a matter of fact, "There can't be anything wrong with my brain. I am too smart."

With her succinct declaration, we dried our tears, gathered our belongings, and headed for the exit. We began a journey of change – individually and as a family unit. These changes extended far beyond our little trio. Everyone who knew and loved us would be touched and changed by our experience.

The clear sunlit afternoon contrasted sharply with the storm raging in our personal world. As we stepped outside the doors of the Medical Tower, Ginger abruptly stopped. She had something important to say. Her words provided a defining moment as we began the fight for her life. "I will beat this. God is not through with me yet."

These words revealed my child's precious heart. Her spiritual depth and maturity far exceeded my own. She exemplified complete trust in God's love and in His purpose for her life. It would be the first of many times she modeled childlike faith.

When my hope ran low, I borrowed hers. When fear and doubt threatened to overwhelm me, I returned to this moment and my daughter's declaration.

How true those words proved to be! No, Ginger, God was not through with you then, and He is not through with you now!

Chapter 2
What Next
One Step at a Time

The English proverb declares, "Familiarity breeds contempt."

Not in my world. For me, familiarity provided comfort. As we walked away from the Baylor University Medical Center campus, I left familiar surroundings, shaken from any perceived comfort zone, for the unknown territory of Children's Medical Center. While I preferred to remain in my secure environment, I knew Ginger needed much more than they could provide.

The amazing staff at Children's Medical Center facilitated our journey through the emergency room and admission process with compassionate expertise. They recognized our anxiety and proficiently addressed concerns. Within moments of arriving, we settled into our new home away from home.

The specialists presented a detailed plan. Ginger required a shunt to relieve the pressure in her brain before any attempt to remove the tumor. They emphasized the urgency and scheduled the procedure for early the following morning.

Once the initial shock subsided, I addressed a number of practical issues. I phoned a good friend to assume my carpool duty.

Ginger's tight circle included sensitive, caring friends. Their parents needed an opportunity to share difficult news in the best way for each of the individual children. Though her illness deeply affected her closest friends, they proved resilient, protective, and unbelievably supportive.

Making calls from the hospital room proved problematic. Each call required sharing our current situation and resulted in an emotional breakdown. Neither of us could speak without dissolving to tears, which kept Ginger in a state of turmoil. "Mommy, please stop crying. When you cry, it makes me cry."

Kerry drove home, made the necessary calls, and returned to the hospital with a change of clothes and toiletries.

The hospital staff distracted Ginger with games and toys. After an exhausting day, she fell asleep. Kerry and I made ourselves as comfortable as possible and spent the first of many nights in the hospital room. A straightforward, practical man, Kerry prayed, asking God to care for his little girl. He exhibited total trust and anticipated a successful procedure and complete recovery.

Kerry and Ginger often tell me I take on the worry quotient for the entire family. They often quote a line from *Steel Magnolias*, "Mom, you worry too much. In fact, I never worry about anything, because I know you'll be worrying enough for both of us." [1]

---

[1] (Harling, 1987)

That evening certainly was no exception. I remember only being afraid and numb. Somehow we made it through the night. Morning came, and we waited for the surgery time.

Our pastor, Dan, and his wife, Marilyn, entered the hospital room, providing a precious illustration of God's love in a very tangible way. They wrapped us in warm hugs and represented God in human form.

Double vision presented as one of the symptoms of Ginger's illness. The previous Sunday afternoon, Ginger reported, "Mom, when we were in church today, I saw two Dans in the pulpit."

As Dan visited with Ginger, he joked, "Two Dans must have filled up the whole front of the church."

She giggled and smiled genuinely for the first time since we heard the scan results.

Before the technicians arrived to escort her to surgery, Dan talked and prayed with Ginger. He spoke simply to her, acknowledging her fears. "We can't go with you into the operating room. Your mom and dad can't go with you but will be in the surgery waiting room. I know you must be scared to go there alone. But you know, you won't really be alone. There is nowhere you will ever go that God will not be with you. God will be there in the operating room watching over you and the doctors the whole time."

Dan asked her to recall her scripture memorization. They recited Psalm 23:4 together. *Yea though I walk through the valley of the shadow of death, I will fear no evil, for thou art with me. Thy rod and thy staff, they comfort me. (KJV)*

When the attendants arrived to escort her to surgery, she bravely left the hospital room without so much as a whimper, assured of the presence of a loving God.

Double doors closed, separating me from my baby and taking her from my protection – a false protection – nothing I did could protect or help her. Nothing in life prepared me for the illness of my child. Empty and helpless, I waited and prayed.

Of all the things I found to worry about, a mass in Ginger's brain never occurred to me. However, nothing surprises God. He knew every detail. Throughout the summer of 1984, He prepared Ginger. Even as a preschooler she possessed a spiritual maturity beyond her chronological age.

When she returned from church camp, she shared concepts and asked questions challenging me to deepen my own relationship with Christ.

Throughout the 1983-84 school year I helped her prepare for Bible Drill, and we both memorized the assigned scriptures. God orchestrated the perfect verses to sustain us. When I lacked the ability to focus enough to read or to pray, I recalled those passages at the perfect time for the exact need.

Ginger paid attention in church and in Sunday School. As she applied the lessons, she taught us all. We learned to believe in miracles as we witnessed one after another.

Children hear stories and apply with a literal understanding. When Ginger returned to her hospital room, doctor's orders prohibited liquid following the surgery to avoid nausea and vomiting. She complained of a sore throat and extreme thirst. She cried and begged for something to drink. "Please, Mommy, I need a drink."

As I stood by the bedside soothing her lips with a wet washcloth, she looked at me and said, "Mommy, can we pray?"

"Sure, sweetie, do you want to pray or do you want me to say a prayer for you?"

Without hesitation, she voiced her prayer, "Dear God, please give me your living water, like the woman at the well, so I will not be thirsty anymore."

Almost immediately she quieted and fell restfully asleep. Through four surgeries and multiple procedures, she never experienced that kind of thirst again. Ginger's memory blocks many of the difficult treatment days. However, when she tells her own story, she vividly remembers this part of her experience. She recalls hearing the story of the Samaritan woman at the well in Sunday School. Her child-like faith assured her and strengthened us. When she asked something of God, He faithfully answered her.

Every day brought new experiences and new challenges. The change in her appearance proved one of the most traumatic. Just a few weeks earlier, she chose to cut her long blonde hair and embraced the stylish shoulder length bob. She beamed each time someone complimented her more mature look.

Knowing the surgeons plan to shave your hair does little to prepare you for the reality of seeing your image for the first time. She woke from surgery with no hair on the left side of her head, an extremely swollen face, and two black eyes.

The temporary shunt created a lopsided shape to her small head. Curious about her appearance, she insisted on seeing her reflection. I preferred delaying this until the swelling resolved. However, she demanded. The trauma of the moment she saw her reflection destroyed her determination and defied description. After her initial torrent of tears, she maintained a stoic demeanor and complied with every request of the medical team without complaint.. Still, she vehemently refused to allow anyone to visit her. Through sobs she exclaimed, "I look like a monster. I don't want anyone to see me like this!"

My boss, the internist, broke through the wall. He walked in the room, took one look at her, called her Cyndi Lauper. "I'm bringing hair dye. You'll look just like her. You're a rock star."

She definitely sported the haircut for it. Embracing a comparison to the 1980's celebrity, she adopted an attitude to match her style.

Her self-imposed isolation didn't last long. A few very close friends visited, but only after careful preparation so they showed no shock or fear. The fear borne in the imaginations of her friends proved worse than the reality. The experience of Ginger's illness as well as the following months of cancer treatment strengthened their bond.

She enjoyed her adult visitors as they doted on her. Being an only child, she lived comfortably in an adult world.

The hospital room quickly filled with flowers, gifts, and stuffed animals. Ginger received gifts and cards from friends, family, acquaintances, and people we didn't know. One particular favorite flower arrangement provided intense interest – a giant balloon and flower arrangement from Dr. Macho and staff – Yes! That really is his name.

The first of many stuffed animals joined the family. Clyde, the gorilla, remained with Ginger through all her treatment and through traumas of junior high and high school. He even attended college. However, he skipped too many classes to earn a degree. He hung out in the dorm, the only consistent roommate Ginger's ever had.

Cards, letters, food, and calls assured us of the love and support of friends and family. Ginger's room became a favorite place for the staff, especially the interns and residents. We enjoyed sharing the pizza and goodies – much more than we could consume. We welcomed the diversion – anything to distract us from the reason for our new location. Ginger particularly enjoyed the students and residents, developing pre-adolescent crushes on the cutest ones.

Entertaining Ginger and dealing with boredom presented a great challenge. Barbara, our dear friend and children's minister, in a stroke of brilliance, brought a surprise basket containing lots of individually wrapped gifts. She instructed Ginger to open only one gift each day. Throughout her illness and recuperation, Barbara kept the basket supplied. One day the gift might be a stick of gum. The next day's gift, a miniature Cabbage Patch, Strawberry Shortcake or Care Bear figure, some of which still reside in a printer's tray with Ginger's treasures. Having a surprise to look forward to every day, helped to focus on something positive. Other friends kept her supplied in music and movies, anything to keep her mind active and engaged. We did whatever it took to pass the time and keep our minds occupied with anything except the mass in her brain.

We entered the waiting time. The shunt relieved the pressure from Ginger's brain, and her physical condition improved. Still the underlying problem remained. We faced a serious major surgical procedure.

What the surgeons referred to as a "cool down" period proved torturous for us as we waited to learn exactly what lay ahead. The doctors discharged Ginger and allowed us to spend a few days at home. We enjoyed the break from the hospital but waited anxiously for the definitive surgery and the outcome.

We hoped and prayed for a benign tumor.

Kerry's favorite picture of his baby girl

1976 - Two years old in the US Bicentennial Year

First Preschool Picture

Chapter 3
Alone in the Storm

Friday, August 31, 1984

We returned to the hospital as instructed for the scheduled surgery.

The doctors expressed concern about Ginger's white blood count and an increased risk for infection. When I signed the consent for surgery the previous evening, I sensed a feeling of utter dread, as if something really wasn't right.

Again, they took Ginger to the operating room. The closing door produced a less traumatic emotion this time. Almost as if my previous experience produced a familiarity making today easier. She experienced less anxiety and waved a calm, confident, "See you, later."

We settled into the surgery waiting room. A large group of friends and family surrounded Kerry and me. The surgeons prepared us for a long surgery – a full day. Less than an hour later, the door opened and the surgical team walked out. Because of Ginger's elevated white count, they made the decision to delay the surgery.

What did I feel? Disappointment? Anxiety? Relief? A feeling of complete peace surrounded me.

People prayed for Ginger, there in the hospital – all over Dallas – all over Texas.

God answered our prayers that day. I felt His Spirit say, "Not yet. Not today. It isn't time."

Labor Day, September 1984

Kerry anticipated Labor Day with as much eagerness as most children anticipate Christmas. The first weekend of September represented opening day of dove hunting season. He and a group of friends planned the yearly outing as a time of male bonding. Every year he spent the weekend shooting birds. For the first time in our fifteen years of marriage he missed the outing. Instead we spent the entire day in the surgery waiting room.

The previous day we signed the consent forms for surgery. This time a compassionate anesthesiologist presented the forms with a comforting analogy. She described the surgical risk in terms I understood. "You take a risk every time you get in a car. You accept the risk because you need to go from point A to point B."

Surgery represented a similar risk for Ginger. We accepted the risk in order to assure any possible continued life and any chance of normalcy. I no longer experienced the sense of dread and I faced the day with peace.

For the third time in a week, they transported her through the double doors. Familiar with the process, she waved her "See you later, Mom and Dad."

Because the surgery occurred on a holiday, the staff scheduled no other surgeries. The holiday afforded flexibility for our friends' work schedule, and a crowd gathered to support us. Our friends and family took over the waiting room. We settled in for the long wait.

Throughout the day, the surgical nurses informed us of progress and assured us things were going well. After a very long day, the surgeons finally emerged from the operating room and escorted us to a private conference room.

We focused our attention on the physician and waited anxiously for him to speak. He exemplified the stereo-typical neurosurgeon, all business and devoid of emotion. He laid out cold, hard facts. He described the pathology report, medullo-blastoma, a malignant tumor with a very poor prognosis. Less than 50% of children with this diagnosis survived five years, and of those, not all remained tumor free.[2] The surgeon stood, walked out of the room, and left us with very little hope.

Our children's minister remained in the room. The doctor dropped a bomb and left her to deal with the spiritual and emotional impact of his words. We sat in stunned silence not knowing what to do next. Barbara followed her first impulse to pray with us. Before I could respond, Kerry exploded. He absolutely did not want to pray. Feeling abandoned and betrayed he angrily responded. "I prayed. I trusted God. He didn't hear me."

MEDULLOBLASTOMA 2018 STATISTICS SURVIVAL RATES IMPROVED TO 70-80% IF THE TUMOR HAS NOT SPREAD TO THE SPINE. IT EFFECTS 250-500 CHLDREN IN THE U.S. YEARLY, AND REPRESENTS 20% OF ALL CHILDHOOD BRAIN TUMORS.

Our friends filled the room and hallway as they waited outside the conference room. Neither Kerry nor I felt ready to face anyone. Barbara stepped out of the room and shared

---

[2] (https://www.stjude.org/disease/medulloblastoma.html)

the devastating report. They all left without seeing us and reassembled at a friend's home to pray for our family. Despite being surrounded by people who loved us, we faced our emotions alone.

Immersed in our individual pain, we couldn't even comfort each other. I found myself drowning in a sea of disappointment, treading water until I regained my footing. Unlike Kerry, I didn't feel God hadn't heard me. I felt He had abandoned and forsaken me.

And I will bring the third part through the fire,
and will refine them as silver is refined,
and will try them as gold is tried:
they shall call on my name,
and I will hear them: I will say,
It is my people:
and they shall say
The **LORD** is my God.
Zechariah 13:9 (KJV)

Chapter 4
Just When You Thought It Couldn't Get Worse

The recovery room nurses kept us well informed of Ginger's condition. They led us to the ICU waiting room and gently guided us step by step through the process. "When Ginger stabilizes and wakes up from anesthesia, we will come find you so you can see her."

Harsh reality greeted us. Parents and extended families took up residence in the large room, respecting each other's territory. We and everyone around us experienced raw, numbing pain and grief.

Many parents lived in that room for days, weeks, even months. Some left the hospital taking their child home, others did not. We shared a common bond – the inherent need to protect our children – and the overwhelming inability to perform our parental duties.

Generalized guidelines set out the rules for the communal space. I wished for a rule book to tell me what to do and how to feel. Instead, I drifted in a sea of suffering individuals, all seeking an anchor.

I settled into an unoccupied corner of the ICU waiting room and struggled to make sense of the raging storm of emotions. I maintained a stoic exterior and suppressed the agonizing screams which desperately strained to escape.

How can I be strong for Ginger and for Kerry? If I let go, I'll dissolve into hysterics and be of no use to anyone. Dear Lord, I do trust you. Please, help me be strong.

The phone rang and a secretary directed us to the double doors, where an ICU nurse met us. She described the environment and Ginger's condition.

A thick bandage covered Ginger's incision, making her tiny head seem much bigger than normal. Though still quite groggy, she recognized us but said very little and drifted back to sleep. For a moment, an uneasy peace settled over me.

She survived the surgery. We have today. This is a long journey. I am weak and about to crumble. Lord, help me take the next step.

A unique phenomenon occurred in the pediatric ICU waiting area. People barely holding themselves together reached out and comforted others. When a new family entered, the community soon shared the necessary details of each story. Temporary bonds formed out of a mutual understanding of our common suffering.

The ICU maintained flexible hours. Either Kerry or I stayed at her bedside all the time. As the days passed, we grew familiar with our new surroundings.

The day following Ginger's surgery, a familiar couple entered the waiting room. Seeing them evoked a flood of emotions. These precious friends, members of our church family, empathized with our pain. They walked back into a room holding so many personally difficult memories. Years earlier, they waited helplessly in this same room as their infant son, nine months younger than Ginger, recovered from heart surgery. He survived the surgery, thrived for several years, and then died at age five. They ministered to us from the other side of grief. They understood the pain –

They wept with us – They sat quietly with us – A comfort more valuable than any words.

A previously unobserved side of Ginger's personality emerged as she regained consciousness. Our introverted, compliant child revealed a combative, aggressive side. She thrashed in the bed, tossing her head from side to side. Kerry feared she might hit her head on the rails, necessitating a trip back to the operating room to control bleeding or something worse. He stood by her bedside and spoke forcefully, "Ginger, be still. Calm down. You have to be still. You're going to hurt your head."

Exasperated, she replied, "I am being still…Give me a break!"

She used the phrase so frequently, the nurses adopted it. "Give me a break!" became the short-term motto in the ICU.

Ginger remembered very little about those days in ICU. However, the memory of one amusing story remained particularly strong. Carrie, a three-year-old toddler, occupied the bed next to Ginger. The precocious little girl discovered how to disconnect certain tubes. The resulting chaos focused the nurses undivided attention on their little patient. Consequently, the nurses called Carrie's name quite frequently.

Because she occupied a bed in close proximity, Ginger assumed the nurses referred to her by her father's name. She proceeded to correct them and in doing so provided comic relief to the unit. She yelled repeatedly and very loudly, "STOP CALLING ME KERRY! MY NAME IS GINGER!"

As hours turned into days, Ginger failed to respond appropriately. Instead she experienced irrational outbursts and incoherent conversations. The physicians suspected ICU psychosis and decided to move her to a neuro-oncology unit. Though physically she seemed to be doing well, the inappropriate responses continued.

When I attempted to restrain her, she clawed at my arms and chest. A normally quiet, reticent little girl, she screamed at the top of her lungs. Nothing I tried quieted her. The things she yelled contained just enough truth to be amusing.

Her neuro-surgeon exhibited an icy, professional demeanor and his bedside manner left much to be desired. His lack of personality irritated Ginger, and she expressed her displeasure with piercing volume. "My doctor never smiles. There is plenty of time to smile. You come back here and smile at me!"

The oncology nurses found her running commentary amusing. Even the neuro-surgery resident appreciated her humor. The big, good-looking, young doctor scooped her into his arms and carried her to the treatment room for a spinal tap to evaluate the psychosis. His compassionate care secured a position as her favorite doctor. During the entire procedure he assured her, "Ginger, I'm smiling at you."

That night Kerry and I stood on either side of her bed. She slept restlessly. Kerry verbalized our fear. "Could they have done something in surgery that caused this? Will she ever be the same?"

As we contemplated the possibility of a permanent change in our little girl, she provided a moment of levity. She curiously examined the Band-aids covering multiple punctures. She bolted upright in the bed and sang at the top of her lungs, "I am stuck on Band-aid, cause Band-aid's stuck on me."

While we laughed that night, we laughed through our tears. No one listened to our fear. When we voiced concerns to the surgeon, he responded, "She is doing quite well. If you'd like I can take you down the hall and show you children who aren't doing well."

This encounter with the physician left me devastated and exhausted. Our interaction confirmed – the neurosurgeon lacked the capacity to offer emotional support. He served the purpose of proficiently removing the tumor. Rallying our emotional and spiritual resources, we turned to our family, friends, and church family. That night I urgently sought answers. We relied on our faith and prayed in desperation for a miracle.

As I stood beside Ginger's bed, I surrendered and experienced a spiritual breakthrough. I wept and prayed, *Dear Lord, I cannot do this. You entrusted this child to me, but she is yours. I trust you to take care of her, and I give her back to you. I can watch her die, but I cannot watch her suffer this way.*

Unknown to me, at that moment a group of our friends gathered to pray for Ginger, Kerry, and me. A lack of sleep left me physically and emotionally exhausted. Ginger ingested very little water and no food for almost a week. The group prayed intentionally and specifically for our needs.

Well acquainted with the hospital chair/beds, I prepared to spend another restless night. I fell into an unusually sound sleep. Ginger and I both slept through the night. I woke the next morning more rested than in weeks.

For the first time since surgery, Ginger appeared lucid and calm. She actually asked for food. Among the deliveries from the previous day, a beautiful fruit basket sat on the counter. She ate only the grapes from the top of the basket.

When she finished the entire bunch of grapes and asked for more, Kerry and I pondered where we might find more grapes.

While we looked for a solution, a hospital volunteer knocked on our door. A stranger, the friend of a friend, came bearing a gift. She carried a basket of fruit with a huge bunch of grapes the most visible item.

A happy coincidence – I think not! I choose to believe the cluster of grapes represented a physical representation of God's love for us. God cares about even the little things in our lives. Imagine our joy – a cluster of grapes arrived exactly on time as the expression of His intention to meet our needs. He loves me!

What changed?

I sincerely believe in my act of surrender, I opened the door to the blessing God always wanted to provide.

Were all our struggles over? Not at all!

Was the rest of this journey easy? Far from it!

That night I experienced a new beginning. I determined to live with a different focus, one I still struggle to maintain. Stay in the moment. Life is short and uncertain. Enjoy it. Look for God's blessings in the little things. He loves us and wants to give us good things.

Do those good things include a night of uninterrupted sleep for which my friends specifically prayed? Does God care about the Snickers candy bars which the nurses told Ginger would make her daddy fat? I think so.

When I let go and let God be God, I surrender whatever it takes. I open my heart and hands so that He can give me what I need. I believe He wants to bless me with whatever it takes.

> The fining pot is for silver,
> and the furnace for gold:
> but the LORD trieth the hearts.
> Proverbs 17:3 (KJV)

Chapter 5
The Treatment Plan

Ginger's psychosis cleared, and her blood counts returned to normal. However, any illusion of business as usual disappeared as the medical team laid out a treatment regimen. Surgical removal represented the beginning of a long journey.

The radiation oncologist presented a slightly more hopeful outlook. "The surgeons removed most of the tumor, leaving only a small portion in the brain stem. They couldn't get the last sliver without putting her life at risk. The good news is radiation will melt away the remainder."

He carefully explained an available research protocol. The clinical trial consisted of two randomized arms. One group of children received a combination of chemotherapy and radiation, while the other group served as a control group receiving radiation alone. Whether she enrolled in the study or not, she required radiation, which provided her only chance of long-term survival.

Kerry considered the information, and quickly formed a negative response. He favored doing the least invasive treatment possible to guarantee Ginger's best health. "They can't tell us what drug she will get, or even if she'll get medication. How does this help her?"

Uncertainty and fear caused me to vacillate between the options. *How will I feel if the cancer recurs, and we didn't do everything possible?*

This situation resulted in a very sound piece of advice – wisdom I shared with others on many occasions. During one of her daily visits, Barbara listened patiently as I agonized over the decision. She waited while I verbalized every thought in my head. When I quieted, she offered, "Gather the best information you can. Make your decision based on that advice. Then don't look back."

After several long family discussions, we opted not to participate in the research trials.

Studies show people in crisis need to hear the same information an average of three times before they comprehend the meaning and its implications.. Even then, past experience, exposure to medical terminology, and knowledge limit understanding. Stunned, we listened as the radiation oncologist and his team detailed the process. The antithesis of the neurosurgeon, this warm and caring physician answered every question we posed. He never rushed us, patiently explaining anticipated side effects of nausea, vomiting, and hair loss. He continued with potential late effects – a probable loss of several inches from her adult height – a possible decrease in her academic abilities – the likely inability to conceive a child. Because so few children survived to adulthood, other long-term effects remained undetermined.

The favorite of our medical team delivered the information factually, never creating false optimism. However, he left us with a glimmer of hope that our daughter might survive. He spoke directly to Ginger and ended the consultation with a declaration. "You're a pretty girl, inside and out. And you know, I think bald is beautiful."

As he prepared to leave the room, he asked "Do you have any questions?"

"I think you've covered everything." I answered, not realizing how much I didn't know.

Naive to the real complexities of cancer treatment, we signed the consent to proceed with treatment. In actuality, we moved forward with a plan for our only viable alternative.

It took several weeks of physical therapy for Ginger to regain enough balance to safely walk without sustaining injuries. She improved daily. Friends, family, and even the medical team referred to her as a miracle child.

Finally, the day arrived for us to go home. Surgery completed and a semblance of recovery achieved, we prepared for the next phase of treatment.

Fourth Grade School Picture

Family Photo 1983

*For you, God, tested us,
You refined us like silver.
Psalm 66:10 (NIV)*

Chapter 6
Home at Last

Everybody wanted to participate in the homecoming. One friend, an interior decorator, completed a project to create a perfect retreat for a pre-teen girl. A group of Ginger's friends decorated her room with banners and balloons. A banner, created by the church youth group and signed by almost every member of our church, stretched across the living room.

Cards, letters, and gifts arrived daily, assuring us of prayers for a miracle. Maintaining a scrapbook of the get well wishes provided a necessary distraction. We soon realized one scrapbook would not be enough.

The loving care experienced in the hospital continued as we resumed life at home. Someone checked on us daily. They supplied food, allowing us to focus on treatment instead of food preparation.

The first nights at home proved difficult for me. During our hospital stay, I slept on a pull-out chair beside Ginger's bed. Each time she moved, I sprung out of bed to evaluate and meet her needs. At home and in our separate bedrooms, I lay awake listening for anything out of the ordinary. Though her balance improved, she remained unstable, requiring assistance to walk. Fear tortured me. *What if she doesn't call me, gets up in the middle of the night, and falls.*

Though I experienced a reasonable fear for her physical safety, an overwhelming anxiety for the future created the real cause of my insomnia. Many nights I survived with less than four hours sleep at any stretch.

We settled into our temporary routine. While Kerry returned to work, Ginger and I developed a schedule. Our agenda included daily trips to St Paul Hospital for radiation therapy, school work, and even piano lessons. We created a schedule and planned for the required seven weeks of treatment. We prepared for an entirely different kind of life.

Nothing in our past experience equipped us for the impending life lessons. The curriculum included basic survival skills and advanced training in suffering and endurance. We reluctantly enrolled in life beyond the classroom.

The first lessons targeted the fundamentals required for Ginger to rejoin her classmates with necessary academic skills. Ginger's recovery revealed some dismaying surprises.

Prior to her diagnosis, she excelled in academics, which she mastered easily. Following the surgery, though she worked diligently, everything regressed. Her normally beautiful handwriting resembled a beginner's scribblings. She struggled with math concepts and failed to recall previously memorized multiplication facts. Tasks which should have taken minutes, stretched into hours. Out of necessity, I became a homeschooling parent. We spent hours at the kitchen table, sometimes Ginger and I alone. Other times the district's home bound teacher joined us.

We accepted Mrs. Daniels as an integral part of our family. Every morning, the compassionate, competent educator arrived at the house for a one-hour session. The student and teacher quickly bonded. Episodes of vomiting frequently interrupted educational instruction. If Ginger felt the urge, she motioned with a prearranged signal and excused herself. Once she recovered, she returned to the table and resumed the lesson.

After each such interruption, Mrs. Daniels affirmed her young student with the phrase, "Adversity builds character. You are building character, Ginger."

One particularly difficult day, Ginger returned to the table and received her affirmation. Weary of the daily ritual, she responded, "Mrs. Daniels, I think I have enough character now, can I please stop throwing up?"

Without a doubt, nausea and vomiting presented the most challenging side effect of radiation. Ginger threw up every day for the seven weeks of treatment. Simply arriving at the radiation facility triggered anticipatory nausea and vomiting. I agonized. *How could anyone possibly survive when eating so little and throwing up everything she ate?*

Prior to radiation, she loved Fruit Loops, her favorite breakfast. To this day, she detests the thought of Fruit Loops as well as most cold cereals. With little appetite and vomiting almost everything she ate, her weight plummeted from seventy-nine to fifty-five pounds. *She's starving and there's nothing I can do about it.*

In my efforts to support my child's nutrition, I prepared high calorie snacks and meals. When we sat down together to eat, she consumed a few bites. I ate my portion and finished hers as well. My irrational response to food failed to support her health and proved detrimental to my own. I gained weight while somehow rationalizing, *If I eat something, I'll feel better. Isn't that why they call it comfort food?*

As days turned into weeks, our resolve weakened. Multiple medications failed to control the nausea and vomiting. We tried eating before the treatment. When that failed, we tried waiting until after the treatment to eat. We attempted distraction and deep breathing exercises. Nothing worked. The side effects seemed to be cumulative – more treatments – more severe side effects.

One especially difficult afternoon, we sat on the bathroom floor. I bathed her little face with a wet wash cloth. As she cried, she searched my face. "Mommy, I've prayed and prayed to God. I asked Him to make me stop throwing up, but He's not listening to me."

I reached for an answer to a problem I didn't understand myself. I answered in the simplest way I could, "Oh, Sweetheart, God is not making you sick. The doctors are doing things to your brain. Those things are making you throw up. Remember, the radiation treatments help to keep the tumor from coming back. If you can be patient, a little while longer, it will be finished."

In a rare moment of clarity, I felt God's presence. He didn't speak audibly or appear to me in a supernatural vision. Rather than dissolve into a puddle on the floor beside my baby girl, I spoke words of wisdom beyond my human understanding. I shared honestly from my heart. "Baby, If I could make it stop, I'd do it. I don't understand why God doesn't make it stop. We can keep asking to make the sickness go away. We can also ask Him to help you get through this hard time."

I wish I could say the vomiting stopped immediately, but it didn't happen. The symptoms persisted every single day. We struggled with the *whys*. We looked for ways to make it better. We continued to rely on God for the strength to endure.

On the last day of radiation, the vomiting ceased.

Music provided a powerful coping mechanism. It comprised an integral part of our lives and helped to restore normalcy. Whether listening, singing, or playing instruments, music played a fundamental role during recovery. Sometimes it helped us celebrate. Other times it soothed raw emotions, expressed pain, and voiced unspoken prayers. It provided diversion, inspiration, and smoothed out some very rough times.

In an effort to restore routine, Ginger resumed piano lessons. Like most students, she disliked practicing but loved the lessons and performing. Her piano teacher agreed to come to the house twice a week. Though we attempted to set aside practice time, academics and doctor's appointments often trumped music. We discovered skills required for piano helped regain some coordination and cognitive abilities.

If nausea and vomiting posed the most distressing physical side effect of treatment, the loss of Ginger's hair and its effect on her self-image caused the greatest emotional challenge.

Bald may be beautiful. Try convincing a ten-year-old – Good luck!

You really do expect it.

The doctor warned you.

Somehow, I held on to a measure of denial. *Maybe, just maybe, she will be the one exception – the one that defies the odds.*

Then reality descended and stripped away any hope of escape.

We passed the three-week mark into radiation treatment. The surgically shaved area of her scalp started to regrow stubble. Just as I convinced myself perhaps she might avoid hair loss, overnight it all fell out – all except for a small area at the nape of her neck. The technicians fashioned a pad of cheese cloth to prevent the cast from rubbing her neck – curiously the only area spared.

This loss proved the most devastating for her and for us. It evidenced an outward sign of the inward illness. One of her most striking features, her long, thick, blond hair, always attracted attention, which consequently compounded the loss.

She hated the idea of wearing a wig and voiced her opposition with lots of reasons, "It itches. It doesn't fit right. It isn't me! It looks so fake."

Instead she chose hats, caps, and headbands – dozens of them – in coordinating colors to match the outfits she wore.

Building self-esteem in preteen girls presents one of the greatest challenges for any parent. The challenge is magnified in a child who exhibits obvious differences from her peers. I spent hours assuring her of the beauty she possessed – outwardly, but more importantly, inwardly.

No matter how much she heard it from me, she wasn't buying it. "Yeah, right, Mom. You have to say I'm beautiful. You're my mother."

I faced an impossible challenge. I needed to prepare my daughter to confront a world without my protection, a world where she endured cruel stares and hurtful, calloused remarks. So, I did the only thing I knew to do, I continued to emphasize her inner character. I repeatedly assured her, "You are amazing. I am so proud to be your mother."

We celebrated milestones. We marked treatment completion day on the calendar and crossed off treatments daily. The end point coincided with election day. Our normally politically complacent family eagerly anticipated election day, November 7, 1984.

Every Friday we celebrated the successful completion of a week of treatment. Celebrations consisted of something simple – a treat, a purchase, or a place Ginger wanted to visit. Regardless of how either of us felt, we made a point to carry out the planned celebration.

Prior to her diagnosis, Ginger and I established a tradition of mother-daughter days. Our events included plays, musicals, museums and restaurants. We decided to plan a special event for the last treatment day.

Every day for seven weeks, we drove past the Anatole Hotel in Dallas. For us it symbolized a place beyond our budgetary constraints – a place we dreamed of visiting someday. We chose the Anatole for our end of treatment celebration and carefully considered every detail.

The day finally arrived. We chose outfits appropriate for a celebration. I remember vividly what Ginger wore. She carefully selected the jumpsuit purchased for the first day of school and dressed in the jewel-toned outfit for the second time. She coordinated it with matching shoes and hat.

We started the day at the polling location, where I placed my vote. Ginger accompanied me to the voting booth and participated in the process – the social studies lesson for the day.

For the 35th time, we entered the doors to the radiation center. The entire staff listened excitedly as she shared the plans for end of treatment festivities. We hugged the staff and said goodbye. "We'll miss you all, but I can't say we'll miss coming every day."

Done! Like graduation day! We did it! Showing up for treatment every day represented a huge accomplishment. We completed treatment!

We proceeded to our celebration destination.

Cute and confident, she walked into the hotel and ordered chocolate ice cream. She ate as much as she could, then promptly visited the restroom and threw it up.

Years later I returned to the Anatole for a breast cancer survivor celebration. I reveled in the moment. As I celebrated with hundreds of other cancer survivors, I recalled the memory of a special afternoon I spent with my daughter. The recollection stands out as an example of celebrating the ordinary and living each moment. For our family, the Anatole remains a symbol of survivorship.

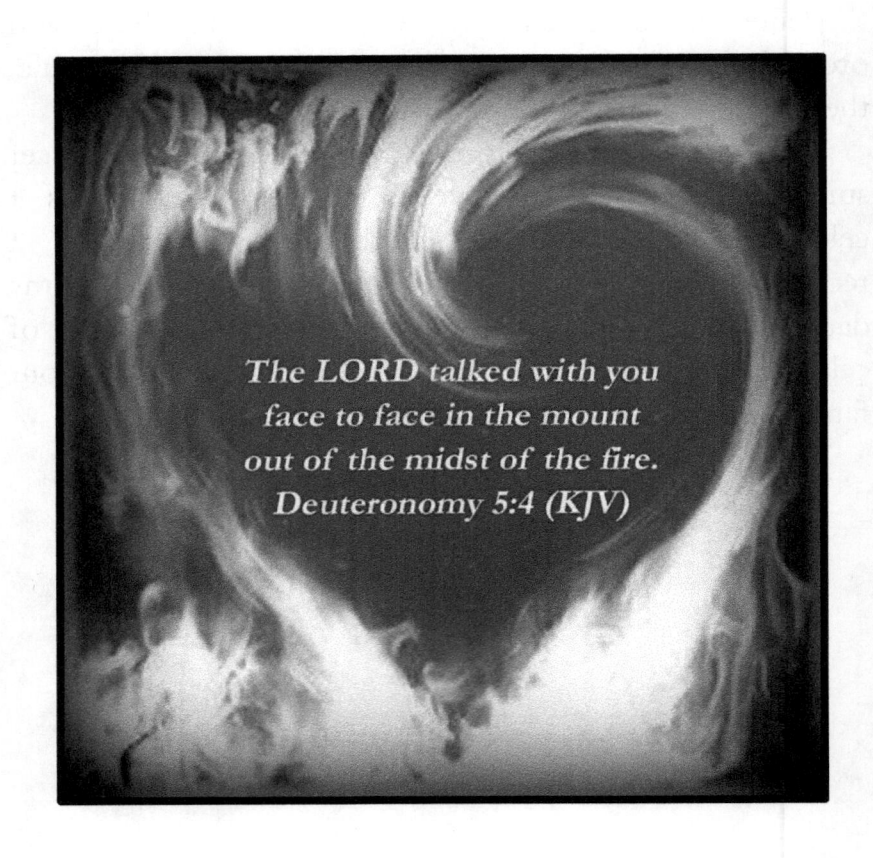

> The LORD talked with you
> face to face in the mount
> out of the midst of the fire.
> Deuteronomy 5:4 (KJV)

Chapter 7
Are We Done Yet?

Wednesday morning dawned with the euphoric anticipation of a day without doctors, nurses, or technicians. No radiation! What would we do with the extra three hours in our new schedule?

Despite the relief and excitement, seeds of doubt crept in my heart. No longer fixated on the daily treatment regimen, my mind wandered to the what ifs. Instead of resuming my normal life, I experienced uncertainty and fear. Constant medical observation and support ended. Nagging questions surfaced. *Is it gone? Did we do enough? What comes next?*

Prior to August 23, I maintained a demanding schedule. I balanced a challenging job with parenting and social activities. Kerry attended college while working full time. Ginger's activities dictated much of my schedule. We juggled school, church, piano, community, and social activities. Suddenly, our world changed.

We entered a difficult time of waiting. No one warned me about the emotions I experienced. Some days I felt elated and life seemed ordinary. Other dark days found me obsessed with questions.

We scheduled a scan for several weeks in the future. The post radiation scan would determine the success of radiation.

If radiation eradicated the residual tumor, our surgeon planned to remove the temporary shunt. If any tumor remained, replacement of the temporary shunt with a permanent one would be necessary.

In the meantime, we waited. Ginger's physical condition improved. The nausea and vomiting subsided, and her appetite returned.

Emotional and spiritual healing proved more challenging. Though I managed to fill my days and occupy my mind with productive activities, anxiety plagued my thoughts. Unanswered questions haunted my sleepless nights – questions which would be answered only with time and experience.

What am I supposed to do now?
Would the cancer return?
When would Ginger be able to return to school?
How would she handle school and social situations?
How will I fill the empty hours?
I'm an entirely different person. When I return to work, where will I find the patience to deal with complaining patients? I have little tolerance for whining. The problems of my patients are important. However, compared to my own, they sure seem insignificant. I can't do the job, if I lack compassion for others.

While the rest of the world slept, I pleaded with God to spare my child and give me strength to live the next day. As my friend Thelma Wells often says, "The meantime is a mean time."

Ginger lacked the stamina to resume most activities. Her susceptibility to infections necessitated isolating her from large groups of people. Because Kerry left the house daily to go to work, most Sundays he remained at home with Ginger while I attended church. It allowed me a break from the daily caregiver stress and filled an essential void in my spirit.

As a young couple, we discovered the large Dallas church on the corner of 10th and Zang. Cliff Temple Baptist Church provided the center of our social and spiritual life. The adults referred to our sanctuary as *The Temple*. With no less reverence, the children simply called it *big church* differentiating it from Sunday School. Built during the depression with sacrificial donations, the striking architecture and beautiful stained glass windows created an awe-inspiring, worshipful atmosphere. Our spiritual mentors encouraged us to explore the scriptures and grow up in our faith.

I carried a heavy burden into *The Temple* on a winter Sunday morning. The cold, dreary weather matched the despair of my soul. Instead of taking my usual spot in the choir, I found a seat near the center of the sanctuary. I wept throughout the message. Dan's sermon emphasized God's healing power. Departing from our normally traditional Baptist service, he invited anyone who needed prayer for miraculous healing to come forward.

As I knelt at the altar, I found myself surrounded by several friends all weeping and praying for the obvious healing need – the permanent obliteration of the tumor and long normal life for my daughter. Beyond Ginger's physical healing, I prayed for healing for my own spirit. I desperately needed healing of the fear and anxiety which resided somewhere deep inside.

When I walked out of the church, the heavy burden lifted. I knew I still faced anxiety-ridden, difficult days. However, I also knew I could trust God with my fears and worries. I left with a sense of empowerment and renewed confidence. Though not audibly, I heard God say to my heart, "I've got this! I've been here all along. I'm still here. I'll continue to hold you as I have from the beginning."

God showed us His love by surrounding us with the love and support of a committed community of faith.

I consistently reminded Ginger, "You are an ecumenical project. Friends from every denomination and faith background are joining to pray for you. People we don't even know."

I found it empowering and comforting to know people prayed for us.

One friend shared, "I keep Ginger's name on my refrigerator door. Each time I pass the door, I pray. Dear God, I don't know what Ginger needs today, but you do. Meet her need today."

We received support in addition to prayers. Friends met our needs on a daily basis. A group of ladies cleaned the house and did the laundry before we came home from the hospital. Some of the guys mowed the lawn. We returned home to a pantry filled with food. I rarely cooked as someone brought a meal every day. Cards arrived daily, assuring us of love and support.

God's people evidenced His care for us. Words fail to adequately express the sincere appreciation for all the ways they upheld us during those tough times.

Being a *type A* personality, the grinding halt to my previously breakneck pace of life proved challenging. However, the slowed pace allowed me to spend time in prayer and Bible study.

One day as I agonized over our future and sought guidance in the scripture, a specific verse leapt from the page and grabbed my attention. Many times, I unsuccessfully attempted to locate the exact reference. It appeared as a promise to me. I read "You will be blessed with grandchildren."

Admittedly taken out of context, I accepted the reference as a message of comfort, "Ginger is your only child. If you're going to have grandchildren, she will survive to adulthood."

The deeper message seemed, "I have a plan for your future and for Ginger's. Whether or not children are a part of that future, trust me. Learn to trust me to care for and supply all your needs. Seek me first and I will give you the desires of your heart."

Our family relationships faced challenges. Kerry, Ginger, and I formed a tight trio – the father-daughter and mother-daughter bond equally strong. Though dependent on both parents, she relied on me to meet most of the difficult physical needs. During my moments of physical and emotional exhaustion, Kerry relieved me. However, when a crisis occurred, she wanted Mommy.

She saw Daddy as protector and disciplinarian. More importantly, teasing, laughing, and playing typified their father-daughter relationship. One day she innocently wounded him by pushing him away. He sent me into her room with a disappointed comment, "I can't do anything for her. She only wants you."

I related to the pain he felt but realized something in their pattern of relating. She associated Daddy with playtime and disassociated him from pain and sickness. Once we accepted her coping mechanism, we approached life differently. We embraced a healthier family dynamic and formed a stronger alliance.

We worked hard to maintain open and honest communication. Through difficult times of crisis, communication and commitment provided the essential keys necessary to remain a strong couple.

Counselors encouraged us to maintain our relationship. They showed us statistics proving many marriages end in divorce after the serious illness or death of a child.

We learned to make important decisions as a family and diligently endeavored to keep the lines of communication flowing.

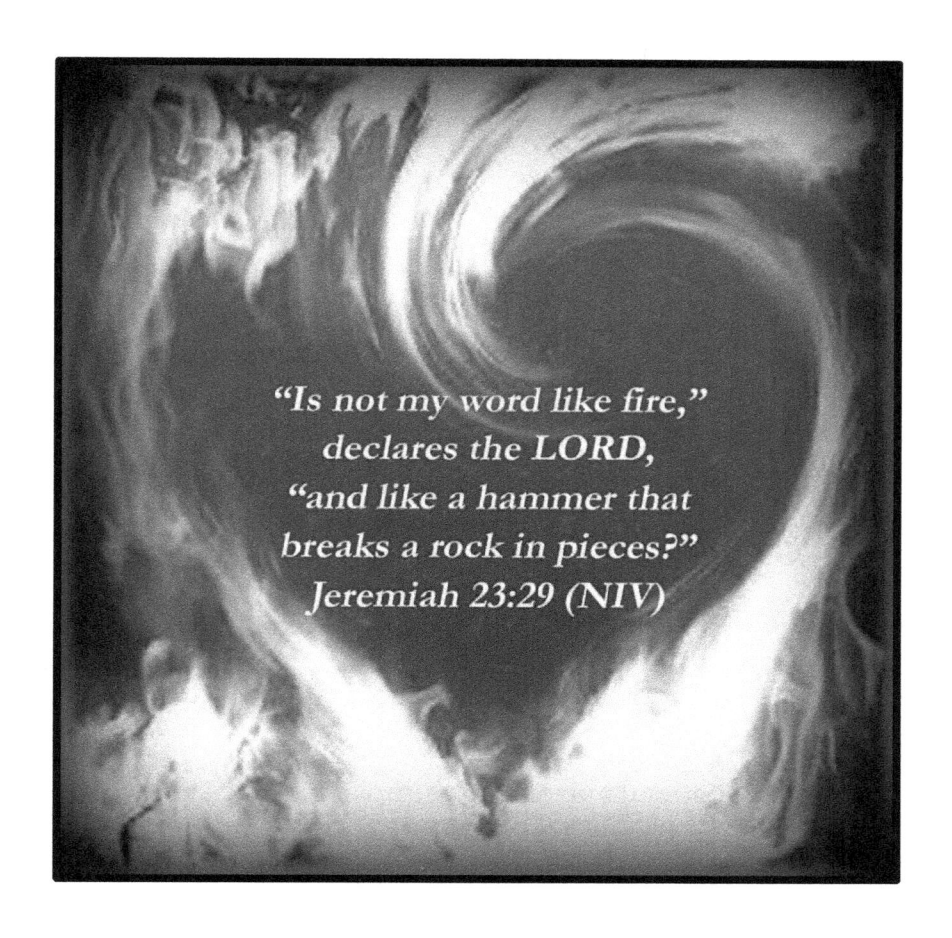

"Is not my word like fire," declares the LORD, "and like a hammer that breaks a rock in pieces?"
Jeremiah 23:29 (NIV)

Chapter 8
Who Knew Shingles Caused Worse Pain than Cancer?

Throughout surgery and treatment Ginger mercifully experienced very little physical pain. We spent mid-November quietly making plans for Thanksgiving and working diligently on school projects assigned by Mrs. Daniels. We eagerly made plans for the holidays, thinking the worst lay behind us.

An outbreak of shingles on her scalp jolted us from our temporary respite. A very concerned pediatrician warned us, "Shingles can spread. If it reaches the eye, it can have serious and permanent consequences leading to blindness."

I nervously watched as each new lesion broke out, spreading down onto her forehead. The last lesions stopped in the eyebrow.

Shingles added insult to injury. Painful sores now covered her bald head. Making matters worse, she developed an allergic rash to the pain medication. A rash covered her face and body and resulted in uncontrolled itching. She further isolated herself, "I look awful. I don't want anyone to see me this way."

The cosmetic aspect paled in comparison to the pain she experienced. In the initial stage, I provided enough pain medication allowing her to sleep through the worst pain.

Once the blisters healed, she experienced shock-like nerve pain, which occurred occasionally. She no longer required constant medication.

The most memorable episode happened during our family Thanksgiving dinner. Suddenly, without warning, a blood curdling scream of pain interrupted our celebration. The pain resolved without medication. We waited until she recovered enough to join us at the table and resumed dinner – a little shaken, yet still hopeful and thankful.

The pain improved over the next several weeks, and she regained her baseline health. Though the lesions left faint scars over her forehead, she escaped permanent damage to her eyes. Another crisis averted.

Again, fear reared its ugly head. I realized each pain and each new ailment presented a challenge to our emotional well-being. Insecurity created constant doubt – How long would it be before I failed to connect even the most minor illness to a recurrence?

*He will sit as a refiner and purifier of silver;
he will purify the Levites
and refine them like gold and silver.
Then the LORD will have men
who will bring offerings
in righteousness.
Malachi 3:3 (NIV)*

Chapter 9
The Most Memorable Holiday Christmas 1984

Christmas afforded us the opportunity to focus on something other than medulloblastoma and everything the diagnosis and treatment involved. We depended on two incomes. The absence of my paycheck stretched our finances. While Kerry's income provided our basic needs – food, shelter, and clothing, we lacked readily available cash for Christmas gifts.

Over the months of Ginger's illness, money arrived at the exact time a specific need arose. Amazingly, God supplied our needs through anonymous gifts, overwhelming us with gratitude. Fortunately, our health insurance covered most of the medical costs, sparing us the economic hardship confronting many families.

We determined to refocus our celebration on the true meaning of Christmas – choosing activities that emphasized Jesus' birthday. We celebrated with our family traditions. We hauled the decorations out of the attic and decorated the house. Customarily, we turned on Christmas music and spent the Friday and Saturday after Thanksgiving decorating the entire house. Decorating took a lot of time and energy, and I loved to enjoy the entire season.

We desperately needed to focus on Christmas celebrations and not the crisis dominating our daily existence. So, we emphasized the familiar, comfortable things, decorating the house and baking Christmas cookies. Instead of singing in the Christmas choir programs, we sat back and enjoyed listening to the music.

Our longest-standing tradition for Christmas involved helping with distribution of Christmas gifts and food to needy families. Even as a toddler, Ginger accompanied me to deliver baskets. Though not wealthy, our middle-class, two-incomes provided our necessities and many luxuries. I determined to model a caring, giving spirit to my child. My efforts paid dividends in her sweet tender heart. She frequently pointed out, "I may be a spoiled only child, but I am not undisciplined."

I recognized a change in my usual focus. Instead of approaching the season with joy and excitement, I felt disappointed and despondent. Completely self-absorbed with my energies focused inwardly, I dealt with self-pity. I wondered, *will things ever be the same?*

The 1984, Christmas season provided valuable insight. I humbled myself and allowed others to minister to me. In early December, a friend called to inquire about Ginger's sizes. She informed me our Sunday School class planned to handle Christmas gifts.

Christmas Eve arrived and with it the gifts. Not only did they bring Christmas gifts for Ginger, they filled our pantry with enough food to carry us through the next months. Grateful tears spilled from my eyes. Without their generosity, Christmas would have been slim. The Christmas celebration took on a deeper meaning for all of us.

The extravagant outpouring of love and gifts from our friends overwhelmed us. It took hours for Ginger to open the many gifts. After our traditional Christmas breakfast, she put on a style show. Pairing each new ensemble with a matching hat, she excitedly posed for pictures in each new outfit. She bounced from one gift to another, unable to decide where to focus her attention. So much!

No subsequent year would ever compete with this.

No tags identified the giver. No one looked for acknowledgement. Each gift represented their love for us – given as an expression and extension of God's extravagant love.

I received the most precious gift – the only one I desired. Surrounded by the love of family and friends, I cuddled with my child and delighted in her happiness.

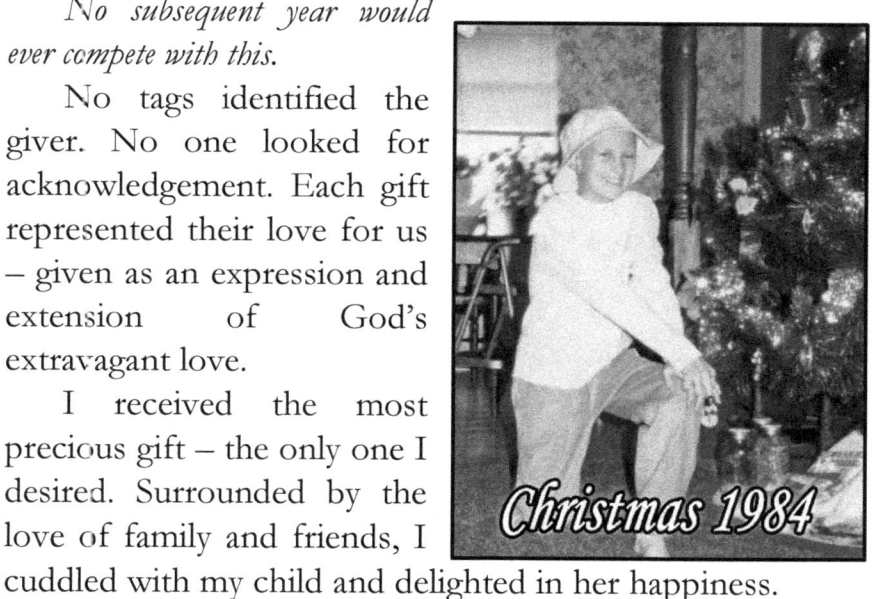

If asked to describe our most memorable holiday, the three of us agree – Christmas 1984 – hands down.

The words of the LORD are pure words;
as silver tried in a furnace of earth,
purified seven times.
Psalm 12:6 (KJV)

Chapter 10
The New Normal

January 1985

We gladly bid farewell to 1984. We eagerly anticipated new beginnings and dared to hope for brighter days. As we approached the new year, old business loomed. The scan appointment drew closer, and my anxiety level escalated.

We braced for bad news. The entourage of physicians and medical students swept into the room. Broad smiles and pleasant conversation signaled a good report – the first really happy news since the initial diagnosis. "The scan is clear, with no residual tumor. When would you like to schedule the shunt removal?"

Anxious to lose the lump on the side of her head, Ginger enthusiastically responded. "Can we do it today?"

The shunt removal required another brain surgery and several days hospitalization. Compared to the other procedures, this procedure seemed minor. Bolstered by the words *tumor free,* even the prospect of another surgery failed to diminish our euphoria.

We officially entered the follow-up phase. Over the next years we returned to Children's Neuro-oncology Clinic for periodic scans and evaluations. Initially, she required close monitoring – after the first year, our quarterly visits stretched to every six months. Eventually, we graduated to yearly visits.

Ginger related well to the staff. She met their questions with honesty and spunk. Her quick, sarcastic wit disarmed the physicians. She challenged them with her determination to overcome obstacles and became a clinic favorite.

"Hello, Mrs. Strange. This is the marketing director for St. Paul Hospital. Dr. M. suggested Ginger as the honorary race starter for our annual fund raiser this spring. Do you think she'd like to participate?"

The typically shy pre-teen surprised me by her eagerness to step into the spotlight. She embraced the opportunity and thoroughly enjoyed the attention. She represented the hospital well. Other opportunities followed and brightened the recovery period.

Ginger loved soccer, especially the Major Indoor Soccer League. She idolized the Dallas Sidekicks, particularly a player known as Tatu, meaning *armadillo* in Portuguese. Brazilian born, Antonio Carlos Pecorari, leading scorer for the league, distinguished himself by ripping off his shirt and throwing it to someone in the crowd each time he scored a goal. A good friend arranged for Ginger to meet her hero, and their picture appeared on the sports page of the Dallas paper – good press for the Sidekicks and a dream come true for a young cancer survivor.

To the medical community, she represented a success story. To marketers, she presented an opportunity for good public relations. To her family and to those who consistently prayed for her, she exemplified God's miraculous power.

The cancer diagnosis changed our lives forever. For months, life revolved around surgery and treatment. Every day brought guests and gifts. Nothing about our life seemed normal. When the doctors delivered the good report – CANCER FREE, we celebrated.

Now what? Cancer changed everything – the way we viewed life – the way we approached activities – the way others saw us. How do you revert to normal after the cancer experience?

We no longer understood what normal looked like. Instinctively, we knew nothing would ever be the same. However, we faced the daunting prospect of finding a new normal.

My heart desired to protect my daughter from ignorance and insensitivity. Unfortunately, I confronted an impossible task.

Hadn't she suffered enough? The illness had taken so much. Why don't people understand and act with compassion?

We moved from the protected world of a hospital where every child shared a similar experience to a world where no one understood the complexities of childhood cancer treatment. The lack of experience limited their ability to relate.

The return to school proved even more traumatic and challenging than I imagined. I attempted to cover all the bases. I spent time with the principal, counselor and school nurse and expected the administration to prepare the teachers for Ginger's return to the classroom.

Each morning I drove her to school, returned home, and waited by the phone in case she needed me.

Despite my best efforts, my worst fears materialized. Though I expected questions and cruelty from middle school students, I never contemplated the events and scenarios which caused the greatest emotional distress. The children proved more mature and supportive than some of the teachers.

Silly me – I expected the principal to prepare her staff. Unfortunately, the teachers remained naïve to challenges their returning student presented. On her first day, Ginger encountered the reading teacher, a stickler for rules and strict enforcer of the dress code. In their first exchange, the stern educator demanded compliance – any headgear violated the dress code. The student complied, removed the bandana, revealed her bald head to the entire class, and dissolved into tears.

My pent-up emotions finally found a target for suppressed anger. Like a protective momma bear, I prepared to attack. Furious with the principal and the teacher, I unleashed righteous indignation. They failed – They behaved insensitively – They lacked compassion. Even though I felt justified in my tirade, I knew the real source of my anger stemmed not from their actions but from an irrational anger and the reality of a situation I couldn't change.

The humiliated teacher apologized to her student, and by the end of the year Ginger and her teacher formed a tight bond.

As I reflected back over the situation and others like it, I realized the need for community awareness, education, and advocacy. I learned the importance of advocates for all cancer patients.

When Ginger returned to full school days, I returned to work. Somehow we made it through the semester. It helped to focus on others and stay busy, though I wondered about the effectiveness of my job performance.

Ginger spent a good deal of her time in the school nurse's office. Physically and emotionally fragile, she often wept because of a heartless remark of a classmate, or a thoughtless comment of a teacher. She found solace as she sat in the lap of the compassionate school nurse.

She approached school with the same tenacity she confronted each challenge. She returned home each day to be comforted and built up in preparation for the daily challenges of her pre-adolescent world without fully understanding how the illness and its treatment changed her. It altered her perceptions. Our family dynamics shifted.

None of us remained the same. The cancer experience colored everything. With an uncertain future, we determined to appreciate small blessings – never taking anything for granted.

No child arrives with a *How To* manual and pre-teen girls employ special rules of engagement. Saying *No* to a child with a life-threatening illness brings an overwhelming sense of guilt. Discipline remains a difficult but necessary task.

At a pivotal point, I realized, *Ginger could survive and live a full life. I don't want her to be an undisciplined, rude adult. I must learn how to apply loving discipline.*

In our one-child family, we incorporated a motto which we stuck with through recovery. Our child, like most American children, might very well be spoiled, but she would not be undisciplined. We set limits and where possible followed the approach of natural and logical consequences. She rarely pushed the limits, making the adolescent years relatively easy.

Far from perfect parents, we made plenty of mistakes. My desire to shield her from any further pain led to my worst parenting decisions. The serious illness of my child heightened the normal maternal instinct to protect. I hovered and overprotected. Little by little, I intentionally loosened my grip and realized the importance of allowing freedom. As I practiced trust in God to care for the details, I released the illusion of control.

A core group of friends surrounded and protected Ginger. They kept her grounded, accepted her, and allowed her to be normal. Like any teenager, she feared being different, and she struggled to blend in. The hair loss made normalcy impossible. During a youth trip I experienced the group's depth of commitment and love for each other.

As the girls stood in line at Disneyland, they observed some girls whispering and staring at Ginger. Being accustomed to this kind of behavior, she ignored the teens and let it slide. Her friends, on the other hand, felt an obligation to deliver a sensitivity lesson. They questioned the girls' manners asking, "She doesn't have hair because she's had cancer treatment. Don't you know it's rude to stare?"

As they matured through their adolescent years, they remained close. They challenged each other to grow spiritually and held each other accountable. In this core group, Ginger found acceptance. They remained friends on the good days and on the bad days. They allowed her to meltdown, when the situation merited it. With them, she could be herself; with or without hair, quiet or rowdy, happy or sad. Genuine friends outlasted the fair-weather ones and matured into caring young women.

The experience of cancer reorders priorities. The concept of limited time puts things into a new perspective. Initially, an introspective evaluation provides the basic framework to make necessary and appropriate decisions. *What is really important? What gives meaning to relationships and life? Is this activity really important? Does it bring me joy?*

When we confronted the prospect of limited tomorrows, many things lost their importance. Today became our primary focus. We embraced the philosophy of enjoying the current moment. We made living each day to the fullest our number one priority.

For several years following treatment we wore ourselves out packing days with activity and making as many memories as possible. It seemed as if Ginger endeavored to make up for lost time. Like her mother, she enjoyed a variety of activities and interests. She observed and emulated my frenzied pursuit of eclectic interests – not because of a perceived deficit, but because she wanted to discover the world.

We sought balance. We worked to provide. We pursued education to learn. We traveled, sang, and read to add joy to our days. We pursued a happy medium between living in the moment with preparing for the future.

A quote attributed to both Eleanor Roosevelt and Bill Keane embraced this life view. "Yesterday is history, tomorrow is a mystery, today is a gift of God which is why we call it the present."

Children's Minister Barbara Crawford and Ginger, Easter 1985

Ginger and Wanda Easter 1986

Kerry and Ginger, Summer 1988

Wanda and Ginger, 1986

Wanda and Ginger, 1992

Piano Recital, 1992

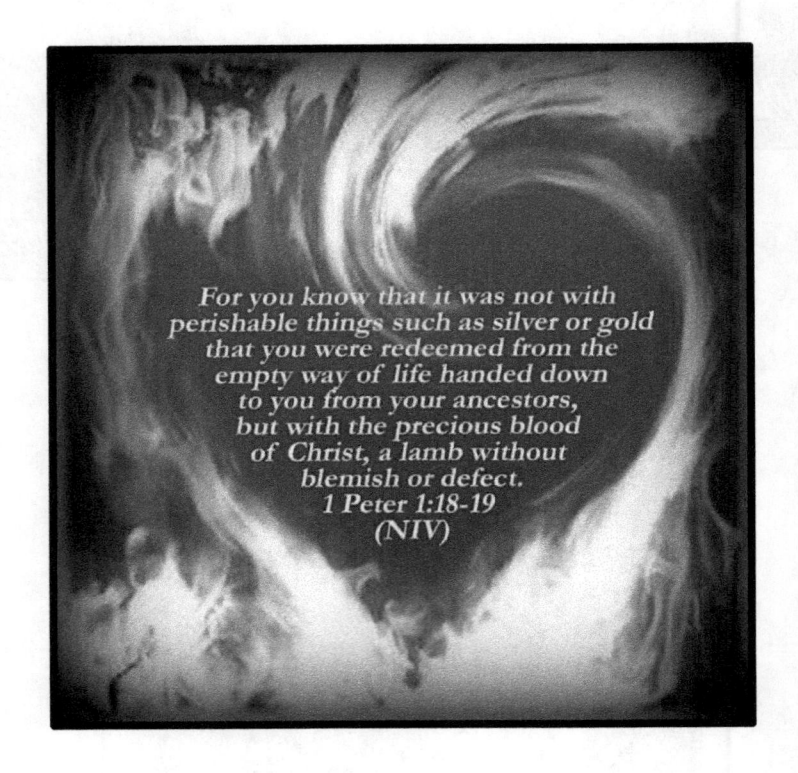

> For you know that it was not with
> perishable things such as silver or gold
> that you were redeemed from the
> empty way of life handed down
> to you from your ancestors,
> but with the precious blood
> of Christ, a lamb without
> blemish or defect.
> 1 Peter 1:18-19
> (NIV)

Chapter 11
Aftereffects

A Bad Hair Day Beats a No Hair Day, Any Day

Several years into her recovery, the junior high English teacher assigned an essay. She instructed the class to write about their worst day. Ginger attempted to write about the day her hair fell out. For hours she tried to put her thoughts on paper. After multiple attempts, crumpled paper, and meltdowns, she chose to write about something less significant and less emotional.

As she absorbed the discussions of her classmates, she concluded most of her peers couldn't identify with a really bad day. The normal concerns of young teens paled in comparison to the toll cancer exacted. "Tell me your worst day, and I bet I can top it."

Most cancer survivors will grow new hair, and we expected her hair to return. After a couple of years, we dealt with a stark realization. She faced the prospect of permanent alopecia. Her reflection in the mirror constantly reminded her of what she lost.

She found it difficult to be gracious when her friends whined about unruly hair. "I'll trade my no hair for anyone's bad hair."

She hated wigs. "They look fake. It's not natural. They're uncomfortable and don't fit."

In her totally honest approach to life, she held the view. "This is me. Take me or leave me."

After years of researching the market, a custom-made hairpiece offered the solution to a natural look. Throughout the years she expressed a desire for her own normally growing hair – one of those prayers that remained unanswered.

However, on her good days, she responds, "You bet it's my hair. I paid lots of money for it."

Why Is School So Hard?

Before medulloblastoma, Ginger learned quickly and mastered academic tasks with ease. After radiation, learning became increasingly difficult. Math presented the most difficult challenge. She required constant redirection to maintain her focus. Every night I tutored her. We worked diligently at mastering the skills she needed to succeed in an academic world.

We persevered and her grades initially remained high, but as time passed, her grades slipped from above average to average. We found most educators supportive. Though since she now looked quite normal, they failed to fully understand why she struggled.

She graduated from DeSoto High School and made plans to attend West Texas A & M. University. The radiation oncologist warned us of the probable drop in her intellectual capabilities. When algebra issues surfaced at college, we sought his counsel. When I inquired about historical data for previous patients, he offered none. "Mrs. Strange, I've never had a patient with a history similar to Ginger's who attempted a college education."

The statistics at the time of Ginger's diagnosis revealed a bleak educational outcome. Only half of the survivors of childhood medulloblastoma survived ten years. None of the survivors attended college. The college advisors granted our oncologist's recommendation to allow Ginger to take untimed testing for her algebra course. She joined a study group and completed the course with a "C". Her pride in passing Algebra surpassed her pride in the higher grades on her college transcript.

She completed a bachelor of science degree in interdisciplinary studies and earned state certifications in education. More than a source of pride, her academic accomplishments serve as a testimony to God's miracles in her life. She lived against the odds and accomplished much more than expected by medical standards and statistics.

Crisis of Faith – Why me? Why now?

After almost twenty years as a childhood cancer survivor, we relaxed into a comfortably normal routine. The pediatric team transitioned Ginger's medical care to a capable internist. The vague awareness of potential long-term and late effects failed to concern any of us, including the physicians. We moved forward – Kerry and I as empty nesters – Ginger as a recent college graduate.

She secured a teaching position and loved her work with inner city children. After purchasing her first car, she rented an apartment and relished an independent lifestyle of a typical twenty-something.

Ginger called me late one summer afternoon. "Can I come over and borrow the computer tonight? I need to print something for my class tomorrow."

Like most teachers, she spent much of the summer attending continuing education classes.

"Sure, I'm leaving work pretty soon. Why don't we meet for dinner? Then you can come to the house and get what you need."

After dinner, she logged on and spent several hours surfing the Internet. Things seemed normal. As she collected her materials and prepared to leave, weird symptoms appeared. Her eyes widened and darted wildly around the room. She repeatedly glanced over her shoulder.

"Ginger, what's wrong? What are you seeing?" I urgently quizzed her to evaluate the situation.

"I see party people." she replied.

"Party people?"

"Yes, they are having a party but it is all black and white," she described details, obviously terrified at the vision in her mind.

The situation quickly deteriorated. She lost function of her left side. Her inability to walk or to communicate clearly horrified me. My calm, take charge demeanor masked the inward panic threatening to render me helpless. "We have to get her to the hospital. I think she may be having a stroke."

As suddenly as with the initial diagnosis, disaster altered our existence. Another life squall shattered the calm evening and quickly intensified to tornadic force winds without warning.

Kerry and I carried her to the car. I sat in the back seat with her, and Kerry sped like a racecar driver to the Baylor emergency room. As the staff accessed her condition, she experienced a full-blown grand mal seizure, the first of her life.

Banished to the waiting room, Kerry and I waited. We communicated without words. Despite our attempts to remain in control, our faces portrayed the terror rising from our hearts. We relived all the agony of the previous twenty years. Past experiences heightened our anxiety. My mind leapt to recurrence. *It's back! The cancer's back!*

The cat scan relieved our initial fear. The doctor delivered encouraging news, "There is no tumor. It looks like perhaps scarring from the shunt, or possibly late effects of the radiation might be the cause."

She spent the weekend in the hospital and underwent additional tests which confirmed the diagnosis. Physicians assured us "Medications can control the seizures. She should be able to resume her normal activities."

Ecstatic, we assumed everything would be fine. We could continue our normal routine. Unfortunately, our attitude proved overly optimistic and naïve.

Life following the seizure presented more challenges than first anticipated. It took months of experimentation with multiple medications to find the right regimen.

She vividly articulated her frustration with her mental status, "I feel as if I'm living in a 12-story building, and my elevator only goes to the 8th floor."

By the end of the summer, Ginger continued to struggle with the after-effects of the seizure. She experienced physical, mental, and emotional trials. Her symptoms resembled those of a traumatic brain injury. Her compromised ability to process information quickly, coupled with hearing loss, affected her job performance. The new administration at the elementary school lacked empathy. A medical leave of absence seemed the only viable option – a leave and attitude that resulted in her resignation.

Anger, anxiety confusion, disillusionment, depression overwhelmed us. *Why now? Why after all these years?*

We stood at a crossroads, experiencing another crisis. I found myself questioning more now. *Why would God bring us this far to let us down? What are we supposed to do with this? What next? If God has a plan for this, I sure wish He'd let me in on it.*

He answered – *Trust me. I am with you. I will never leave you.*

Oh no! Not again!

Eventually, we fell into a quasi-normal routine. Employment issues continued to plague her career. Ginger drifted from one position to another, searching for a job with accommodations for her deficits.

One Sunday evening, we attended a July 4th concert in Stephenville before returning to our Dallas apartment for the work week. We enjoyed the music and thought about nothing in particular as we drove through the city.

"Mom, slow down. That car is trying to get over."

"What car are you talking about?"

"I'm in trouble, Mom." she uttered in a hushed tone. At the same moment I realized no car occupied the lane she indicated. We both recognized the symptoms and knew what to expect. I breathed deeply to calm my quickening pulse. *I must remain calm and get us to the hospital. I have to get help!*

As I approached downtown Dallas, I accelerated and sped to the Baylor Hospital emergency room. I bolted from the car and grabbed the police officer in the ambulance lane. Within a few seconds a team transported her through the doors. Before they got her in a treatment room, she suffered her second grand mal seizure.

Aspiration pneumonia complicated her recovery from this episode. She spent a week in the hospital recovering. The neurologist adjusted the seizure medications. The use of hormones for the management of a gynecological condition caused her to experience this seizure.

Although she responded favorably, the cumulative effects of radiation and seizures exacted an additional toll.

She worked hard to overcome the deficits. The natural trait of tenacity served Ginger well. Determination, time, patience and support allowed her to regain much of her function and resume a productive life.

Again, we questioned, *God, I don't understand. Why? What next? How do we conquer another unsurmountable obstacle?*

Again, the only answer, *Trust me. I am with you. I will never leave you.*

Socioeconomic Challenges

Congress enacted federal laws with provisions to protect cancer survivors from discrimination or loss of insurance coverage. However, to avoid pre-existing penalties, continuous coverage must be maintained without any lapses.

Insurance and employment presented a significant challenge. Between jobs, Ginger managed to maintain insurance, though she spent all her savings to do so. Each job loss threatened insurance loss, the ability to pay for expensive medications, and obtain necessary medical care.

After the last seizure, the administrator at Texas Oncology helped me submit paperwork to add Ginger to our insurance as a disabled adult dependent. After medical review, Blue Cross Blue Shield approved the application and I carried her on my insurance until my retirement date. Once I retired, she obtained coverage through the Affordable Care Act.

Though federal law prohibits job discrimination against cancer survivors, it would be naïve to believe it never happens. While no employer would be bold enough to terminate a person because of cancer, limited protection exists if the employee misses work for treatment or illness. Long-term effects of treatments often leave the survivor with deficits affecting the ability to perform certain job functions or pursue certain career paths.

In 2016, Ginger applied for Social Security Disability. We worked with a third-party advocate to complete the necessary paperwork. They requested medical records, scheduled her for a hearing evaluation, and extensive neuropsychological tests. The reviewers denied the initial application.

My journal entry from November 15, 2016 expressed the depths of depression in the midst of the application process.

It's been a while since I wrote in this prayer journal, and I expect this to be a lengthy entry. Thank You, Lord, for provision and Your intervention. I confess my doubt and despair. Last night was about as low as I've been in a long time. I wondered, and I questioned.

I know You are leading me to write difficult things. Last weekend I felt your guidance, and You spoke to me through Lisa and Beverly. I submitted. But, Lord, You know it was a reluctant, "Okay, I'll do it."

I could not have known what was coming – but I am beginning to understand. It is about giving up control and letting go. I know the lessons are still to come. Make me willing to listen. Yes, this is about Ginger. But it is also about me – about my stubborn desire to "fix" everything.

Lord, forgive me – Forgive my doubts – Forgive my obstinance.

It is not lost on me that I discovered the SS deposit just before midnight. Even though a super moon illuminated the night – my soul remained dark. I watched helplessly as Ginger struggled with the pain of being miserably unhappy with her life. Like every mother, I want to make it better. Here we sat debilitated and immobilized by depression. I ache for her – for what she feels – I hurt for myself – realizing my dreams for her and her dreams for herself need to change. We need a new dream!

I'm not sure how or if the money from Social Security will change the circumstances. It will provide a route to some new possibilities.

I love You, Lord, and I praise You for showing me love and patience. You are good — You provide — I trust You. Help me trust You more.

Again, His answer. *Trust me. I am with you. I will never leave you.*

> I counsel thee to buy of me gold tried
> in the fire, that thou mayest be rich:
> and white raiment, that thou mayest
> be clothed, and that the shame of
> thy nakedness do not appear:
> and anoint thine eyes with
> eye salve, that thou
> mayest see.
> Rev. 3:18
> (KJV)

Chapter 12
Emotional and Social Issues

Changing Labor Day from Dread to Celebration

"Will September ever come and I won't feel this way?" I asked this question of a psychologist friend one evening when I felt particularly down.

"Yes, but it will be a very long time," she replied with wisdom and compassion.

For years I approached late August and early September with a sense of dread. The first few anniversaries surprised me. After some difficult experiences, I learned to anticipate the time of year and plan something special to counteract the depression.

Kerry celebrated Labor Day like most people celebrated Christmas. He loved dove hunting. He carefully planned a yearly outing with a group of good friends. They escaped and spent "male bonding" time.

Early on, Ginger and I appreciated the chance to enjoy some mother-daughter time. We eagerly anticipated the weekend with the same excitement as Kerry's enthusiasm for the annual boys' trip. We looked for ways to connect, communicate and do the girly things we enjoyed but Dad tolerated.

Each year Labor Day provides an opportunity to celebrate life as a survivor. My friend's wisdom proved true. Instead of approaching September with despondency, I look forward to a celebratory event.

Combating Isolation

Even though family and friends loved and supported us, we still felt a sense of isolation. I longed to connect with someone who lived through similar circumstance and survived. I yearned to see one child who thrived after surviving treatment. I felt as if no one really understood the fear and anxiety or the issues we confronted.

Worse than my sense of isolation, I watched as my daughter endured emotional pain. I tried to be sensitive to her feelings. She resisted any attempt to involve her in a support group. Instead, she gathered a close-knit group of friends. Though they loved and supported her unconditionally, they lacked the energy and maturity to understand her agony. The depth of her pain created isolation.

Ginger recognized her differences. She wanted to belong and shunned anything that caused her to stand out. She tried to blend in – certainly she avoided anything emphasizing her differences.

The cancer experience included us in a club to which we neither desired membership nor filled out an application. You would never invite your friends to join this exclusive club. Though others shared similar struggles, ultimately, we all confronted the demons alone.

The Pity Party

We call it the *pity party*. You throw these parties alone. You invite no one, and no one comes.

You enumerate all the reasons your life sucks!

You cry because things aren't the way you want them to be.

You talk to God and tell Him all the things you feel. As if He doesn't know, you tell Him all you've been through.

You ask, "Why? Why me? Why now? Why don't You fix this? What did I do to deserve this?"

Sometimes a word from God comes – either through His Word, through a friend, or through quiet reflection.

Sometimes God is silent.

At times, He simply wraps you in His love and you hear Him speak to your spirit, *I know*.

Other times, you look inward or sometimes in the mirror and the answer becomes clear.

Life is a gift! For as long as my life lasts, I will choose to live it in gratitude. I will find ways to share my experiences and my life in a way that brings glory to the God who gives me life and who sustains me.

> As the fining pot for silver,
> and the furnace for gold;
> so is a man to his praise.
> Proverbs 27:21
> (KJV)

Chapter 13
Celebrating Life

As a little girl, I counted the weeks until spring and summer vacations and the days until Christmas. As a teenager, I looked forward to graduation, followed closely by a wedding.

No matter how fulfilling the career, most workers eagerly anticipate weekends and vacations. We look for opportunities to celebrate.

During Ginger's treatment and recovery, we developed multiple coping mechanisms. Celebrating small victories and milestones proved one of the most valuable.

Every day became a celebration. Yeah! We made it through today! We counted down to the end of radiation or whatever current challenge we faced.

Throughout the first year, we approached every holiday as if it might be our last one together. The net benefit resulted in many over the top festivities. Viewing each day as an opportunity to celebrate life heightened the little joys and minimized minor annoyances. We faced the challenge of maintaining a joyous attitude. Everyday life with its minor agitations threatened to cloud the joy we wanted to experience.

Ginger's life-long best friend, Frankie, introduced us to a way to joyfully express gratitude for the gift of survival. The American Cancer Society's Relay for Life[3] ignited my passion for survivorship.

I prepared myself for strong emotions as I observed the survivor's walk. I stood stoically with my team and watched the parade of cancer warriors clad in purple shirts. I beamed with pride as I watched my daughter round the track. *Yeah! I made it through without tears.*

Relay for Life is a team fundraising event where team members take turns walking around a track or designated path. Each event is six to twenty-four hours in length. Each team is asked to have a member on the track at all times to signify that cancer never sleeps. Cancer patients don't stop because they're tired and for one night neither do we.

Then I saw her. The crowd continued to cheer as the last participant crossed the finish line. Her daughter and son supported the older woman on either side. If she dropped out along the way, only a few would notice and no one would judge. She lagged far behind the group. She plodded along, determined to complete the course.

This precious lady moved me to tears. She and others like her inspired me. She typified the spirit of survivors. She reminded me why I chose to end my career in oncology.

---

[3] (https://www.cancer.org/involved/fundraise/relay-for-life.html)

Survivors keep going when it would be easier to give up. They celebrate milestones along the way and encourage others by their example.

Many brave individuals and their families honored me by allowing me to share challenges and celebrate victories. As we journeyed, they taught me to revel in the ordinary moments of life.

May 2004, presented a momentous milestone for Ginger. We discussed options for her thirtieth birthday celebration.[4] As with many young women, she expressed dread, "Can we just skip this one?"

Fortunately for Ginger, I recalled the irrational emotions accompanying my own landmark birthdays which kept my plans for the festivities under control.

"Seriously? Ignore your birthday? I don't think so. You can choose how to celebrate, but doing nothing is not an option."

A celebration is a special enjoyable event that people organize because something pleasant has happened or because it is a birthday, or anniversary of a special event.

The celebration of something is the praise and appreciation which is given to it. ie: This was not a memorial service rather it was a celebration of life.

We settled on a low-key celebration. Several weeks following her birthday, Ginger experienced an *Aha* moment. After some soul-searching, she emerged from a well of self-

---

[4] (www.collinsdictionary.com)

pity. She felt guilty about whining over her status as a thirty-year-old single woman and declared, "I'm turning my attitude around. Instead of moping and moaning, I choose to celebrate twenty years of cancer survival."

Her friend, Frankie, and I jumped on the opportunity and planned a memorable event. We decided to surprise Ginger with the celebration. We left no detail to chance. Kerry left for his annual dove-hunting trip. Frankie, Ginger and I traveled out of town for a weekend excursion, including shopping, dinner, and a live show. Ginger returned home, completely satisfied with the weekend anniversary commemoration.

Monday morning, Amy picked Ginger up for a cousin's day out. With Ginger happily occupied, Frankie and I decorated and prepared for the party. Everything worked perfectly. Many of the people who supported us through Ginger's illness gathered to celebrate. We pulled off the biggest surprise of her life. Love and support overwhelmed her.

What a wonderful evening! We celebrated her. We recognized the miracle God worked in Ginger's life and in our lives through her cancer experience. Seeing God work in and through Ginger touched many people. Over the years we observed her childlike faith. As she confronted additional struggles, her faith matured. Each of us grew spiritually as we witnessed and recognized God's miraculous healing and provision. A card from her childhood friend, Randi, said it best, "Your life is proof that God hears and answers children's prayers."

I love celebrations! Holidays and birthdays provide a reason to party. I enjoy decorating for each season and every holiday and look for reasons to host gatherings of family and friends. I open my home for any occasion and love making the event special for the honoree – holidays, birthdays, a wedding, a new baby, an anniversary, promotions, accomplishments, changes in the seasons, sunrise, sunset, or just hanging out together – any excuse for a party.

I especially enjoy springtime with the promise of new life and new beginnings. The beauty of spring evokes grateful praise to God the creator. Bluebonnets and wild flowers carpet the Texas fields, hills, and roadsides. Every year I plant flowers with a sense of hope.

Maybe I'll be a more successful gardener this year than last. Even if I don't succeed it will be pretty for a little while.

Most of all spring heralds Easter. I anticipate Easter more eagerly than Christmas. As much as I love everything about Christmas, I prefer Easter because it commemorates Christ's resurrection. Easter frees me to celebrate every day of life on earth as I look forward to the promise of eternal life in heaven with Christ.

My heart desires so much more than simply surviving. I want to thrive. Life is meant to be cherished and celebrated. God intends us to have an abundant life. Jesus tells us, *The thief comes only to steal and kill and destroy: I have come that they may have life and have it abundantly. John 10:10 (NIV)*

The New Living Translation of this verse reads, *that they may have life and have it to the full.*

Abundance means a great supply, having more than enough. God desires for us to live in abundance – more than just enough – more than merely existing. He provided beauty in nature and a world of incredible wonders. He blessed me with a wonderful family to love and be loved in return. How dare I waste time and allow anything to steal my joy!

The dictionary defines full as occupying all of a given space. When I fill my life with bitterness, anxiety, past hurts, and anger, I leave no room for joy, peace, patience, and kindness. Each person has a choice – God's best, an abundant life, focused on the blessings – or allowing the thief to choke out the best, getting us to settle for a life of simply surviving.

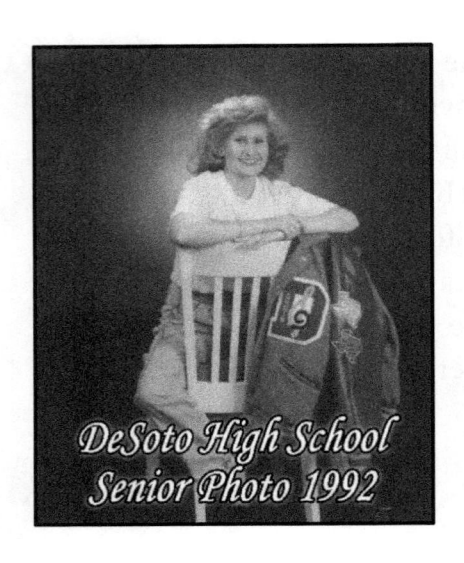

DeSoto High School
Senior Photo 1992

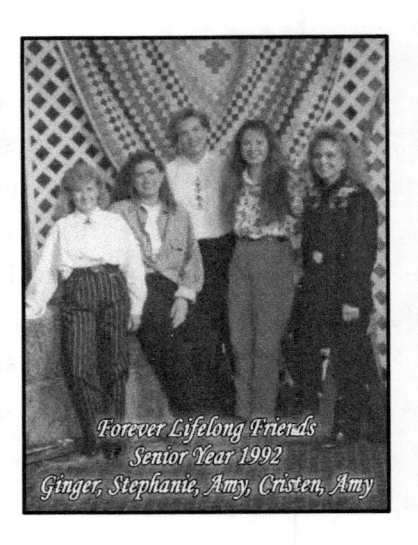

Forever Lifelong Friends
Senior Year 1992
Ginger, Stephanie, Amy, Cristen, Amy

Loving Family -
Mawmaw, Amy and Ginger
Around 1994

Emerging from the Crucible

College Days - Back Home for Easter
About 1996 Cristen, Ginger, Amy, Amy

Forever Friends - Amy and Ginger

Another Family Celebration 2017
Wanda, Jenni, Lisa, Ginger, Amy

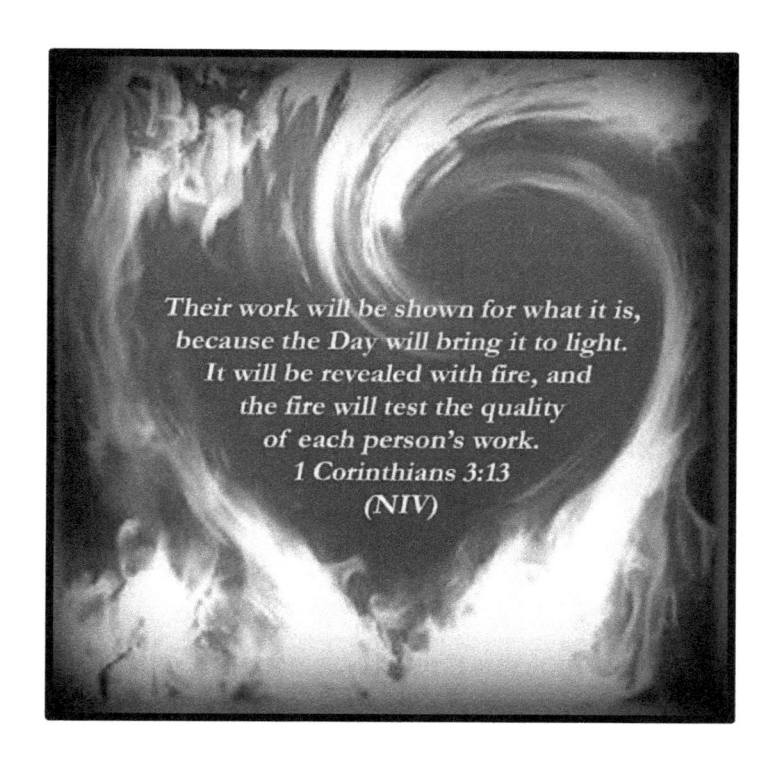

> Their work will be shown for what it is,
> because the Day will bring it to light.
> It will be revealed with fire, and
> the fire will test the quality
> of each person's work.
> 1 Corinthians 3:13
> (NIV)

Chapter 14
Post Cancer
Changing Perspectives

My Professional Journey

March 1999, I walked into an office at Baylor Sammons Cancer Center and discussed my qualifications and skills with the administrator. The entire interview I wondered *What am I doing here? Who am I kidding? I can't do this?*

Everything in me screamed. *No way! No how! Not me! There is a laundry list of reasons why this is a really bad idea! I've been the caregiver, and I would get too emotionally involved. I would burn out quickly. It will be depressing. It will hurt too much to watch people I care about suffer and die. The list went on and on.*

God has a sense of humor! He has a marvelous master plan! Just tell Him something can't happen!

I spent the final two decades of my career as an oncology nurse for U.S. Oncology, the last six years as an oncology nurse navigator at Mary Crowley Cancer Research Center.

My patients taught me and contributed far more to me than I ever provided for them. I played a small role in the lives of patients, aspiring to help each one achieve the best quality of life possible for as long as possible. Though some common threads bind us together, each individual and each family brings something unique and special to the cancer experience. Though cancer still claims far too many lives, many long-term survivors continue to live full lives.

God called me to oncology nursing. He saw in me something I failed to see in myself. He gave me a heart for hurting patients and their family members. He used my experience to cultivate me into a passionate advocate. I became a voice for patients in the workplace, with insurance companies, and anywhere I saw the opportunity to raise awareness of survivorship issues.

God used my patients to show me true courage and teach me how to fully live each day. I accepted a call to make a difference in the lives of cancer patients and their families. Their lives intertwined with mine affirming the difference we made for each other.

I worked alongside many fine professionals who agree – oncology nursing is the hardest job you will ever love.

Changes in Kerry's Career Path

Kerry enrolled at Cisco Junior College immediately following high school graduation and fully enjoyed the college experience. His grades reflected the lack of priority assigned to class and studying. He described his consternation at the school's decision, "I'm still trying to figure out why they didn't invite me back?"

Consequently, he spent the next few decades pursuing a trade in the sheet metal industry. The physical challenges of his job caused him to re-evaluate the need for higher education. With his characteristic sense of humor, he explained, "I decided to use my brilliant mind instead of my brute strength to make a living."

With determination, he completed six hours a semester while working full time. Ginger's illness interrupted the pursuit of his education. Part of *normal* for our family included college classes. After a one semester break, he resumed the quest for a Bachelor's Degree and achieved the goal of being the first in his family to graduate from college. His parents beamed with pride as they celebrated the accomplishment with us. Our entire family shared in the success. I often quipped, "I should have my name on that degree. Can I get college credit for all the papers I edited and typed? Do I get recognition for helping with study and research?"

During the decade following Ginger's illness, Kerry continued to work in the sheet metal industry. When the economy declined, Kerry found himself at a crossroads. A job loss and life experiences led him to a mid-life career change. One night he presented a concept that took me totally by surprise, "I think I would like to try teaching."

I responded, "I think you've lost your mind. You love your child. You tolerate her friends, but you really don't like kids. Why would you want to spend your days doing something so totally out of character?"

After much discussion, I suggested, "Why don't you try substitute teaching? If at the end of a year of substitute teaching, you still want to pursue a career in education, we will do whatever it takes to make it happen."

Kerry agreed. He spent the next few years obtaining an alternative certification and completing a Master's Degree of Education.

The decision changed his life. He found a calling. He spent the last twenty years of his career working with inner city teens. Teaching required commitment and provided rewards beyond a paycheck. Kerry summed up his love for teaching and for his students, "The greatest joy results when I encounter a former student in the community or one of them returns for a visit. The young adult reports he or she is doing well, and in some small way acknowledges the difference I've made."

How Cancer Changed Our Marriage

After the diagnosis of a serious or chronic illness or the death of a child, statistics indicate that a significant number of marriages end in divorce. One or both parents may devote all their attention and time to the child and neglect the marriage relationship.

In 2018, we celebrated forty-nine years of marriage. Our commitment to God, to the marriage, and to each other sustained us through the tough times. Rather than driving a wedge, sharing the pain forged a bond between us.

Kerry's sense of humor and quick wit diffused many difficult situations. Our opposite temperaments, interests, and communication styles served to make us stronger. Through times of individual firestorms, we allowed each other space to experience emotions and find our own equilibrium. We learned to depend on each other, appreciate our differences, and find common ground. When one faltered, the other stood firm.

The reality of our shared experience challenged us to live in the moment as much as possible. Kerry encouraged me to let go of small aggravations, release anxieties, and celebrate the present. He chose the philosophy, "Most things people worry about never happen. Those that do happen I can't change anyway. So, why worry?"

I benefited from my husband's gift of embracing the present and living in the moment. Before Ginger's illness, many crazy things consumed my thoughts, and I worried about a lot of things. None of those things ever happened. It never occurred to me to worry about a brain tumor.

Mark Twain wrote, "I've had a lot of worries in my life, most of which never happened."

Those crises that knocked me to my knees blindsided me. Worry didn't change the situation and I couldn't control even the smallest detail.

An Always Evolving Perspective

Cancer changed our perspective and philosophy. We gained membership in a society we never wanted to join, and the group continues to grow. Since Ginger's illness, many friends and family members joined the club. I faced my own battle with breast cancer. We lost Kerry's dad and my dad to lung cancer, and my step-father to colon cancer. Other diseases claimed lives of those we loved. Kerry's mom died of emphysema, his sister of heart disease, my mother from complications of diabetes. A unique sense of grief, loss, and pain accompanied each death.

However, no other single event compared to the life-threatening illness of my child. Though I would have never chosen this journey, it changed me for the better. It drew us closer, forming us into a tight-knit unit. Because of the cancer experience, each of us developed positive character traits and made us stronger individuals. Ginger's teacher, Mrs. Daniels, was right – adversity does build character.

I embraced Friedrich Nietzsche famous quote, which I first heard in a line from *Steel Magnolias*, "That which does not kill us, makes us stronger."[5]

What about Ginger? Life Goes On

Ginger articulated as she shared a diagram drawn in response to a recent Bible study assignment. "Every time I climb out of one cistern, another one pops up. They're all related to the big one – the cancer. Still, each one is different and presents another challenge."

As we considered the Biblical illustration using Joseph as an example of how to face hard times, Max Lucado's video assured us *You'll Get Through This*. Over several weeks we dared to re-examine wounds. Some we expected to be healed, others we knew still elicited pain.

He encouraged us to compare our difficult situations to the life struggles of Joseph. His brothers threw him into a cistern and sold him into slavery. They caused the situation. His difficult situation resulted from their bad decision and evil intentions.

The current assignment: *Reflect on the cisterns in your life. Ponder who had a hand in putting you there. How was God with you through the dark time? Have you seen God use this experience for good? How has the experience shaped you?*[6]

---

[5] (Harling, 1987)
[6] (Lucado, 2013)

Hard questions without easy answers – *Who can you blame for cancer? Why do bad things happen to good people? Is God good when life isn't?*

When each challenge, disappointment, anger and despair surfaced. *Why? Is this not enough? What else? Will this never end?*

Far too often, we felt like the old testament character, Job. After every devastating loss, I heard Ginger's desperation. I wept with her. I listened one night as she poured out her heart and voiced her pain, "God, what else can you take from me?"

Then I observed her resolve and strength as so many times before. She trudged through the days. Together we searched for a solution.

After watching Ginger rebound from so many disappointments, I wondered, *How does she keep bouncing back? How does she keep from giving up?*

I prayed. *Dear Lord, Give us strength and wisdom. Please lead us to the best solution. Most of all, don't let us give up. Help us trust You, no matter what.*

Despite one challenge after another, Ginger rebounded and thrived. She set goals and worked *diligently* to achieve each one. She completed a degree in interdisciplinary studies at West Texas A&M before her twenty-second birthday.

Celebrating Completion of the Master's Program

Concordia Graduation

She graduated with high honors (4.0) and earned a Master's Degree in advanced literacy from Concordia University. She pursued additional training to work with children who experience reading difficulties.

Between crises, Ginger enjoys a relatively ordinary life, engaging in many of the same activities as her peers. She seeks ways to discover and accomplish her life's purpose.

She spends a lot of her free time with children. While physical challenges limit her career options, she continues to modify her work environment. Working with children who struggle to read and seeing their progress rewards her efforts. While she often lacks patience with herself, she exhibits the trait with her students.

Teaching preschoolers in Sunday School, Awanas, and Vacation Bible School fulfills her calling to work with children.

Ginger turns spectator sports into an interactive physical experience. She particularly enjoys Dallas Stars Hockey and Dallas Mavericks Basketball. Watching games with her exhausts me. I sometimes remind her, "The players cannot hear you, no matter how loud you yell at them."

An avid movie buff, Ginger favors *chick flicks* and frequently watches her favorites until many of the lines are committed to memory. She excels at movie trivia and loves to challenge others with her knowledge of actors, roles, and favorite quotes.

Music also provides a source of joy. Though she enjoys most genres, hit songs of the eighties comprise the majority of the play list.

Her competitive side emerges when she engages in board games.

Ginger cultivates a giving spirit and chooses to support causes that benefit children. Remembering Christmas 1984, she never misses the opportunity to give back. Each year the two of us shop for the wish list of a specially chosen child from the local Angel Tree Ministry.

Another family Christmas tradition includes shoe boxes for Samaritan's Purse Operation Christmas Child initiative.[7] We spend quality time choosing the perfect combination of items to fit in a shoe box and pray for the child who will receive our boxes.

---

[7] (HTTPS://WWW.SAMARITANSPURSE.ORG/OUR-MINISTRY/ABOUT-US/)

> *Samaritan's Purse is a nondenominational evangelical Christian organization provides spiritual and physical aid to hurting people around the world. Since 1970, Samaritan's Purse has helped meet needs of people who are victims of war, poverty, natural disasters, disease, and famine with the purpose of sharing God's love through His Son, Jesus Christ. The organization serves the church worldwide to promote the Gospel of the Lord Jesus Christ.*

Because she understands the challenges of childhood cancer, she contributes regularly to St. Jude's Children's Hospital.

With accommodations and adaption, life looks fairly normal. Ginger desires the same things all people want – love, acceptance, health, purpose. As she faces each new challenge, she modifies her goals and dreams and keeps moving forward.

So, we return to the diagram of Ginger's cisterns. When she finds herself at the bottom of yet another one, she struggles. As a human being, she sometimes expresses anger and disappointment. Since the anger has no tangible target, depression and despair lurks.

Unlike Joseph, no one put her there, so there is really no one to blame. Certainly, nothing she did caused the situation. The smooth, damp walls of the cistern make it difficult if not impossible to climb out. If we are fortunate, all of us aren't imprisoned in the cistern of discouragement at the same time. As long as one of us remains outside the well, the other can offer a rope and a hand up.

Over more than three decades, God proved faithful. Though doctors predicted a survival rate of less than fifty percent, Ginger not only survived, she thrived. The cancer experience and the resulting challenges shaped Ginger's faith and her character.

Though life threw some pretty nasty curves, she celebrated more than forty-four years of life. August 2018 marks thirty-four years of survival. In every dark place and difficult situation, God kept His promise.

Graduation Celebration With the Family

Best Friends for over Forty Years

Cousin Amy, Ginger, and forever friend Frankie

Celebrating Stewardship

Forever Friends - Amy, Frankie, Ginger, Randi

> But who may abide the day of his coming? And who shall stand when he appeareth? For he is like a refiner's fire, and like fuller's soap.
> Malachi 3:2
> (KJV)

Chapter 15
The Future Versus Living in the Moment

If you could see into the future, would you really want to know?

When I held my newborn daughter, would I have wanted to know the difficulties our future held?

Would knowing the challenges ahead of our family have changed the way we lived the first ten years of Ginger's life?

Absolutely!

The fear and anxiety would have crippled us. Normal discipline of my child would have been impossible. Could all the anxiety change the outcome? Not by my human efforts!

If God controls the universe, can I trust Him to take care of my life and all its problems – big and small?

Bad things happen to everyone. Every person on planet Earth participates in their own story, some more dramatic than others. God never promised a life without heartache and pain. To the contrary, He assures us of the trouble to come. *These things I have spoken unto you, that in me ye might have peace. In the world ye shall have tribulation: but be of good cheer; I have overcome the world. John 16:33 (KJV)*

The good news – He controls the world!

The Bible clearly encourages us to focus on today and not to be afraid. *Fear not! Don't fret! Don't be anxious. Don't worry about tomorrow.*

Jesus instructed us not to worry. He admonished – not suggested – rather He commanded. *Therefore, do not worry about tomorrow, for tomorrow will worry about itself. Each day has enough trouble of its own. Matthew 6:34 (NIV)*

Today is yesterday's tomorrow.
What happened to all those tomorrows that became yesterdays?
How did I spend them?
Did I use them to ease someone else's hurt?
Did I share an encouraging word?
Did I miss opportunities to be God's hands in the world?
These questions haunt me.

Each day dawns without the promise of tomorrow. Those people who touch my life today may never cross my path again. No one else shares my exact experience. Kerry's and Ginger's perspective on the same events differ. God uses our unique personalities and experiences. Life presents us with opportunities to touch and inspire the different people we meet.

When I reflect on my day and recognize the opportunities I missed, I feel drained and conflicted. If I follow my calling and make myself available, I realize one person can make a difference. As I fulfill my purpose, I live an abundant life.

Every successful event requires organization and careful planning. As we plan, we show responsibility for the resources God entrusts to us. The dynamic tension exists – finding the balance between planning ahead and enjoying the present. When we spend all our time and effort planning for the future, we risk losing the joy of today.

God has a plan for His children. My Creator knows me better than I know myself and understands my strengths and weaknesses. He challenges me to glorify Him in both. God promises a plan for my bright future.

For I know the plans I have for you," declares the LORD, "plans to prosper you and not to harm you, plans to give you hope and a future. Then you will call on me and come and pray to me, and I will listen to you. You will seek me and find me when you seek me with all your heart. Jeremiah 29:11-13 (NIV)

What a precious promise! No matter what I plan for my life, I trust God's more excellent plan. I don't want to miss anything He plans for me. I want to experience it all!

> For our God is a consuming fire.
> Hebrews 12:29
> (KJV)

Chapter 16
Lessons from the Cancer Experience

Life Is a Gift!

On the day my daughter arrived, I acknowledged her life as a precious gift. For years, I begged God for a child and prayed for her even before her conception. I acknowledged her life as a precious gift – a priceless treasure.

The cancer experience heightened my appreciation of her life. I recognized the fragility of life. Following Ginger's diagnosis, we identified ways to celebrate life and treasure time together. We focused on building strong relationships – with each other, as well as with family and friends.

As a child, my parents taught me to say *please* and *thank you*. Throughout my life, anytime someone gave me a present, I said, *Thank you*.

On the hardest days, my gratitude consisted of the ability to simply put one foot in front of the other, but I continued to look for reasons to be thankful. I developed a practice of expressing gratitude and reaped indescribable benefits.

God gives us many gifts. When I express gratitude for the gift of life, my awareness of the many other blessings He provides intensifies. Each sunrise represents another opportunity to live fully. I choose to embrace life with an attitude of gratitude!

I Can Control Nothing!

A self-confessed control freak, I struggled with letting go. Over the years, I tried to fix things for Ginger and for Kerry – a habit which resulted in driving them a little crazy. Despite evidence to the contrary, I clung to the concept *I can fix this! Whatever the current "this" might be.*

My first-born characteristic of maintaining control of my circumstances drove my attempts to solve everything for everyone around me. Failed attempts served as proof of the illusion. I possessed not a single ability to control anything.

Despite my bests efforts, I cannot change the situation. I can only try to control the way I respond to it.

Consistently, I return to my Heavenly Father, present my mess, and ask Him to do whatever it takes to make things right. When I completely surrender my life, He guides my decisions and continues to work in all things for my best. He provides peace and assurance.

The Most Important Things in Life Are Not Things!

Many people spend much of their time and energy acquiring stuff. Because our society values stuff, our homes, cars, and material possessions signify success and security. We often speak of the things we need. It seems the more assets we acquire, the more we need or want.

I enjoy a nice home, drive a decent car, and choose food from a well-stocked pantry or freezer. I own an abundance of things – more than I need and most of what I want.

A quick inventory of my home reveals objects which belonged to our parents and grandparents. Though none of these items represent significant economic value, each relic reminds me of the people to whom they belonged. Being the sentimental sort, I hold them a little too tightly. The memories represent the only true value assigned to any of these possessions.

I realize I really *need* very few things – a roof over my head, clothes to keep me warm, and food to eat.

No monetary value can be placed on the things which provide my greatest joys – witnessing a sunrise or a sunset – the steady rhythm of waves rolling onto the beach – collecting seashells – the sweet smell of spring rain – the aroma of fresh cut grass – wild flowers – children at play – mighty oak trees – butterflies and hummingbirds – and so much more.

Material things pale in comparison to the time spent with family and friends – sharing – playing – making memories. The best times and greatest memories don't involve things at all.

I bequeath a legacy to my family and friends – not a financial one – but a legacy of faith and love – and hopefully, a lot of really fun memories.

People Display an Incredible Capacity for Giving!

Individuals exhibit an incredible capacity to care deeply. They use their resources to meet needs. People who may or may not know each other combine their abilities to provide what a single person could not.

Allowing Others to Help Blesses Both You and Them!

It is often easier to give than to receive. Pride stands in the way of accepting help. Refusing an offer of help robs not only the person who needs the help but steals a blessing from the giver.

Friends and Family Are What Really Matters!

When I consider the difficult times, I cannot imagine surviving those times without my family and my close friends.

Lifelong friends prayed for us when we could not pray for ourselves. Friends supported us emotionally, spiritually, and financially when we were unable to do it for ourselves.

The bond forged by the experience of Ginger's illness made sisters of her friends. They became surrogate daughters and their parents became surrogate family.

Though time and distance may separate us, our shared experience transcends surface relationships. Tethered together, we count on each other for support in the crises of our lives.

Healing is a Process!

True healing began when we reached out to someone else. About two years into Ginger's recovery, the staff at Children's Medical Center asked us to visit a young girl and her mother. During the crisis of treatment, the mother and daughter sank into hopelessness and discouragement. The physicians thought we might encourage each other.

We accepted the request. We understood the challenge. Returning to the hospital brought back painful memories. Ginger's introverted nature added to the angst. Despite some misgivings, we visited and shared our experiences. Within a few days, the girls returned to their separate lives and never saw each other again.

The brief contact proved therapeutic for us. When we stepped outside the victim role, we moved to another level of healing. For the first time, we allowed our story to encourage someone else.

The Memories You Make Become Your Legacy!

Today is the only day I have. I will make it count.

I take a lot of pictures. Photos provide a visible reminder of the memories we make.

Traditions remind us of where we come from and help us feel grounded. They provide a sense of comfort and stability – some things we always do, like the breakfast casserole I prepare every Christmas morning.

We remember the times spent playing cards or other board games. I visualize my mother-in-law teaching her grandchildren how to play spades.

I recall the laughter around the table as the competitive group yelled the colors and directions for Uno.

The tradition of making Christmas cookies and candies conjure memories of my mother and grandmother in the kitchen.

I sure wish I could have one more piece of my mother-in-law's chocolate pie. No one makes it quite like hers. The granddaughters sure wish they'd learned how to make that special recipe. They swear she left out a key ingredient when she wrote it down for them!

Making a Living is Necessary –
Making a Difference Gives Meaning to Life!

Did I make a difference?

Does what I do every day matter?

Is there meaning to my work beyond earning a paycheck?

Though the income from a career provides necessities of food, clothing and shelter, most people search for purpose beyond the daily routine of a job.

According to a 2017 Gallop poll as many as 85% of people hate their jobs.[8] Perhaps few people view their work as meaningful or as a means to accomplish their calling. The dictionary defines *calling* as a strong inner impulse, or a particular course of action especially when accompanied by conviction or divine influence. If more people worked in professions that allowed them to fulfill their purpose, they might find their labor more satisfying.

Long before the cancer experience, I followed my calling to nursing. Once I found oncology nursing, I realized my passion – a demanding career offering intangible rewards.

My personal experiences with cancer allowed me to empathize with patients and caregivers.

---

[8] (https://returntonow.net/2017/09/22/85-people-hate-jobs-gallup-poll-says/)

Every experience in my life provides the opportunity to make a difference in the lives of people I encounter. Yes, I can make a difference and what I do really matters.

God Can Bring Beauty from All of Life's Experiences, Even Cancer!

Why do bad things happen to good people?
Why does an innocent child suffer?
If God loves us, how can He allow evil in the world?

These questions without easy answers and beyond human comprehension often cause a crisis of faith.

Life is hard! I believe with all sincerity that the loving God I serve does not will illness and pain in our lives. We experience suffering because we live in a broken, fallen world marred by all kinds of disasters.

We prayed for a miracle. More than three decades of cancer free survival evidenced God's miraculous power. God proved faithful to sustain us through the most difficult circumstances.

Our experiences cultivated relationships. Our love for each other strengthened. The bonds with family and friends deepened.

We developed the ability to appreciate life more fully and to empathize with the suffering of others.

My unchallenged faith grew exponentially during Ginger's illness. I learned to rely on God for provision, wisdom, and hope. I observed the changes in other people's lives as Ginger's story touched them.

I Should Thrive Not Simply Survive!

Being a survivor carries with it the responsibility to do something with the life God allowed me to continue. He has a plan for my future as well as the future of those I love. He continues working in and through me, refining me, to fulfill His purpose.

While Prayer May Not Change the Situation, It Does Change Me!

Prayer may or may not change your situation.

The path to healing may take an unconventional route. God may exercise His power to heal miraculously. I believe He can and does.

At other times, He uses the medical community to bring the needed healing. Surgery, chemotherapy, immunotherapy, and radiation therapy provide necessary tools to eradicate some cancers.

As human beings we find it hardest to comprehend and accept when death and heaven provide the ultimate healing.

No matter how healing comes, and though we may not get the outcome we desire, prayer changes our perspective from the finite to the eternal.

I Can Depend on the Presence of God!

Nothing can ever separate us from the love of Christ. In the calm seasons of life, my self-sufficient spirit rises. I can handle day to day life. I conveniently place God in a box.

I got this, Lord. You don't need to concern yourself with my petty little annoyances.

Then the storm disrupts life and destroys my confidence. An event beyond my control requires a miracle. I need God. Not the God I placed in a box – I yearn for the God of unbridled power, peace and joy. The crisis prioritizes my dependence on God.

I recognize my need and pray, *I am undone. I have no resource but You. Lord, Please help me!*

My story of cancer's effect on our family emphasizes our reliance on God. When my human strength falters, I recognize the presence of God more fully. *I can't but God can!*

While Ginger's illness represents my hardest trial, life presents challenges – some related to cancer – others simply related to life in the real world. Challenges prompt me to earnestly seek God. Far too often, I wait for the crisis before seeking God's guidance. Why don't I seek him for the small things, too? *He has the answers – He is the answer – in good times as well as bad!*

The frantic pace of life distracts my heart and mind and thwarts my spiritual growth. I struggle to learn what spiritual discipline and practicing the presence of God looks like in my daily life.

Long commutes in heavy traffic provide a stressful facet of suburban life. Rather than grousing about the traffic and delays, I consciously decided to reflect on the skies and listen for God to speak to my spirit.

As I drove one morning, a bright ribbon of light connected my car to the sun. The traffic stalled, and I focused intently on the brilliant rope of light, which like an umbilical cord, attached me to the sun.

Suddenly, a semi obscured my view of the streaming light. I likened the experience to my view of God's presence in my life. Like the sun, God is constant, always available. In the same way the truck hid my view of the light, problems obscure our view of God.

Often the things that obstruct our vision aren't bad — perhaps a momentary distraction.

Had the light been there before? Absolutely, though I never noticed it. In my rush to get to work, I focused on other things.

When I changed direction, I lost sight of the light. The sun remained. Its rays shone on my car, but my focus changed. When I looked for the light, it reappeared.

Some days I give God my full attention and I feel His presence in everything I do. Other days the busyness of life distracts me and I go about my life as if I control my destiny. Though I avoid overt evil, distractions of ordinary life divert my attention to worldly pursuits. When I neglect spiritual disciplines, I lose my focus and fail to feel His presence.

God does not change. He is constant, the same yesterday, today, tomorrow., and forever. My actions make the difference. When I change my focus and move away from Him, I cheat myself out of the blessing He provides.

We easily take for granted the presence of the sun and depend on its consistency. On days when the sun shines brightly, I reach for my shades to block its brilliance. Looking directly into sun causes pain and possible damage to my eyes, so I look away.

Encountering God's light in the unrepentant areas of my life causes me to squirm painfully under the scrutiny of holy truth.

On gloomy, overcast days clouds hide the sun. Even if I can't see the light or feel the warmth of the sun, I never question its existence. Because of previous experience, I know I will see the sun shine again.

Nature relies on both sunshine, clouds, and rain. Without rain, nothing flourishes and grows. The most beautiful sunrises and sunsets occur when the sun shines through the clouds. The sun's reflected light produces breathtaking beauty.

I rely on God's presence even when I don't see Him. He works in my life even when I don't feel Him. He reveals His glory when I allow Him to work through my difficult circumstances and shine through the dark clouds of my life.

God Supplies Sufficient Grace for each Moment!

John Claypool shared his own discovery of God's grace in *Tracks of a Fellow Struggler*. During his eight-year-old daughter's battle with cancer, he gleaned truths from *Isaiah 40:31. But they that wait upon the LORD shall renew their strength; they shall mount up with wings as eagles; they shall run, and not be weary; and they shall walk, and not faint.*

These words and Claypool's application to the cancer experience became my life line. Some days our spirits soar and we celebrate. We rejoice in the good reports and seize every opportunity to enjoy symptom free moments.

Other days filled with busy activity require the ability to run from one appointment or treatment to the other.

As a parent stands beside the bed of their critically ill child, neither of these actions seems appropriate. On those most difficult days, God supplies the greatest gift. His grace allows us to simply walk – to put one foot in front of the other – to keep on keeping on.[9]

Scripture Sustains – Memorize It!

In the darkest days of Ginger's illness, I found it difficult to concentrate enough to read anything. I often recalled memorized scripture at the exact moment I needed it.

Often, I opened a card or note and found comfort and healing in the printed message. I clung to the hope promised in these words.

Teach your children to *hide God's Word in their hearts. (Psalm 119:11)* and memorize it with them.

God's Word spoke to my heart and gave me wisdom for specific situations. It carried me through difficult times.

Knowing God's Word adds wisdom to life altering decisions and provides comfort in the hardest times.

God Is Faithful!

God keeps His promises. He never promised life would be easy. However, He assures us of His presence.

When I could see nothing but darkness, I experienced His presence beside me in the gloom. I found the promise in Romans 8:26 to be true, *"the Spirit prays for us with groanings too deep for words."*

---

[9] (Claypool, 1974)

When I came to the end of my rope, He reached down and assured me. In my spirit I heard him say, "Take hold. Hang on, my child, I have you and I won't let go."

He promises a peace beyond human understanding. God is faithful! If He said it, He will do it!

Daddy and Daughter 2018

Wanda, Ginger and Kerry, Easter 2018

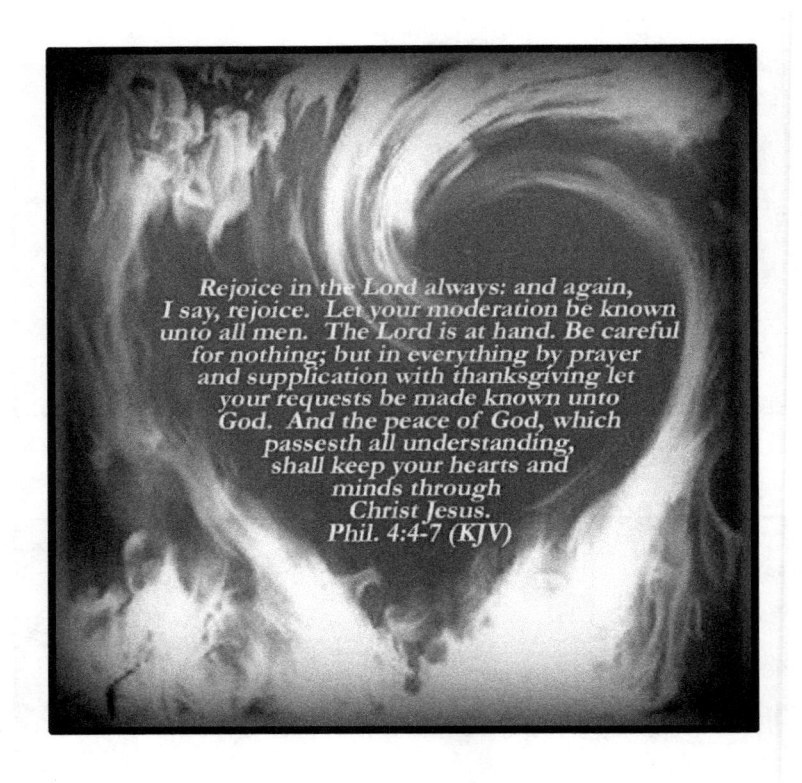

> Rejoice in the Lord always: and again, I say, rejoice. Let your moderation be known unto all men. The Lord is at hand. Be careful for nothing; but in everything by prayer and supplication with thanksgiving let your requests be made known unto God. And the peace of God, which passesth all understanding, shall keep your hearts and minds through Christ Jesus.
> Phil. 4:4-7 (KJV)

Chapter 17
Glorifying God
Throughout the Fire Storm

Is God good when life falls apart?

Can God be glorified even when He doesn't provide the answer or the miracle we desire?

How do I allow His presence to shine in the darkest places?

In *Daring to Hope*, Katie Davis Majors shared her crisis of faith and hope. She opened her home to a Ugandan family. As she physically cared for a young mother with AIDS, she pleaded with God to spare her friend. As the woman's condition worsened, Katie prayed and held firm to hope of miraculous healing. She fully expected God to intervene and restore Katherine to her five children. When her friend died, Katie struggled to understand.

"What do you do when you believe for life and ask for it with all your heart, yet your friend still ends up dead and sealed up in a coffin? What about when you go home from the hospital in the wee hours of the morning and her children are asleep in your living room and you wonder what you will tell them, what you will tell your own children who prayed and believed with you? What do you do when God doesn't show up in

the way that you asked Him to? What was all that hoping for if this was to be the end?"[10]

Oh, how I identify with Katie's questions and with her despair.

One afternoon, my co-worker and friend stepped into my office and closed the door behind him. My office provided a safe haven for unburdening emotional weight of an oncology research practice. Fresh from an encounter with a patient, this typically quiet, stoic nurse broke down.

He asked, "Can you go talk to him? I just spent an hour picking up the pieces in the wake of the doctor's bad news. The treatment isn't working and we have nothing else to offer. I introduced the possibility of hospice, but he doesn't want to consider it."

Over a period of several months, the two men built a strong connection. They shared a common faith. The patient talked openly of his belief and trust in God to heal him. Hundreds of Christians prayed for his healing.

"If I accept hospice, I am admitting defeat. I am saying I don't believe God's power. My greatest desire is to glorify God. He can only be glorified if others see his healing work in my life. No, I can never stop fighting this cancer."

Though this man spoke with confidence of his hope for eternal salvation, he clung to life with determination – and believed God could only be glorified by his physical healing on earth.

The experience saddened us.

We declare, "God is good all the time. All the time God is good!"

Do we *really* believe it?

---

[10] (Majors, 2017)

Even when the news devastates us, do we *really* trust God to sustain us?

Can we reflect God's light through our darkest circumstances?

Over decades in oncology, we observed so many patients and caregivers who glorified God through lives marked with unimaginable pain and suffering. These brave individuals impacted the world as they traveled from this life to eternity.

Through my years in oncology, I met countless, diverse personalities who inspired others with their positive attitude and determination. They exemplified the motto, "I have cancer. Cancer does not have me."

When faced with a diagnosis of metastatic breast cancer, Laura, a young wife and mother, determined to live every day to the fullest. And live it she did!

While showing up for treatments, she maintained her work schedule as well as a busy social calendar. She taught everyone around her the value of remaining in the moment as she poured love into her family and packed a lifetime of living into a few short years. Words from Laura's blog lightened the somber mood and inspired others, "Cancer smancer life goes on."

No matter how difficult the day, Sue flashed a smile, lighting up the room. When the hospice nurse phoned to notify our office of Sue's death, she reported an extra detail beyond the usual clinical information. "Mrs. S died with a smile on her face."

When I spoke with her husband, he expounded. "You know how Sue's smile was contorted since the stroke? The moment she died, her face lit up and her broad smile was perfectly straight. Absolutely perfect."

The night before her death Anita attended church and encouraged a group of young mothers. She returned home and spent the night in meaningful conversation with her husband. He left the room for a moment and returned just in time to witness her passage from her earthly home to her heavenly one.

Her husband described the ethereal glow surrounding her face as she sat up in bed, looked heavenward, and exclaimed "Oh, my!"

Barbara witnessed to everyone who entered her hospital room about God's grace and the joy awaiting her in heaven.

Despite his own failing health, Adam served his church and community by repairing their homes and baking treats for them. He sought ways to share his inventions and shared wisdom borne of a lifetime of experiences. He taught the medical staff the importance of seeing everything that made him *Adam,* instead of focusing totally on his disease process.

The week before he died, Gerald painted the sanctuary of his church. His death caused the entire clinic staff to mourn. The professionals who cared for him echoed the sentiment, "I can't believe it. He was doing so well."

The morning before his unexpected death, he tolerated the treatment well and somewhat uncharacteristically made a point to speak to each staff member, thanking individuals for their part in his care. He and I discussed his pride in how well the Texas Rangers played the previous evening. He showed me pictures of his garden, his family, as well as the interior of the newly painted church.

When faced with the knowledge of her illness, Ethel determined to fulfill her bucket list. In her seventh decade, she jumped from a plane, rode a jet ski, experienced her first hockey game, and camped on the beach. She spent the last month of her life celebrating sunrises on the beach.

I met Alex the day of his daughter's first birthday. "I just bought a video camera. I want to record moments for my daughter, just in case I don't make it."

With those words, he moved into my heart. For over a decade, we shared stories about our lives. He embodied hope. American Cancer Society named him a Hero of Hope. He lived in a hope for the present and as well as the future.

His oncologist often commented, "He left more heart in the surgeon's pan than most people are walking around with."

Despite the heart they removed, Alex had plenty of it. A naturally extroverted young man, he made friends everywhere he went. He loved his family and friends deeply. Always one to have the last word, he chose to create a video for his memorial service. The declaration of his faith in the goodness of God inspired everyone present to live fully, while we continued to fight for a cure.

Kyle dealt with sarcoma for most of his adult life and died much too young at age 38. If you spent five minutes with Kyle, you knew him. His genuineness shined through his larger than life personality. People felt comfortable in his presence. He provided me with one of the most meaningful experiences of my career. In his last days, he made a point to speak to his close friends. One morning, he sent a message asking me to come visit his hospital room. He honored me by including me in those people to which he spoke during his last days.

I stood beside his bed as he spoke words of gratitude. "Thank you for caring for me and my family. You helped me to have more time with my children. For that, I can never thank you enough."

I walked away from the encounter knowing why I chose oncology nursing, or more appropriately why it chose me.

The printed program for Kyle's memorial service glorifies God. His wife, Darla, included a poem which perfectly described their journey.

On a miserable day during the worst of chemo in 2007, I wrote a spin-off of Rudyard Kipling's "If" for Kyle to cheer him up. He read it and flashed me one of his 1000-watt grins. I hope it makes you smile. — Darla Ogle

If... for Kyle

If you can do more with one arm than most can do with two,
If you can smile though the reasons are few,
If you can face suffering with courage and grace,
And not begrudge others who aren't in your place,
If you can look at the odds and know they're against you,
But fight even harder because "lose" is not in you,
If you can count your blessings in the midst of pain,
And refuse to give up, even with little to gain,
If you can trust God when things don't go your way,
And remember that Heaven is just a breath away,
If you can face a world obsessed with perfection,
And know you are complete, no matter the reflection,
If you know life is short but that it can be wide,

And you grab onto it and make the most of the ride,
If you can look Death in the face and still grin,
Then no matter the outcome, I say you win.

Printed with permission of Darla Ogle

Can God be glorified through suffering?
Jesus answered the question with His own life.

As He prayed in the garden, He knew what the future held. He suffered humiliation, physical pain and ultimately death. When He asked for another way, God answered with silence. He didn't promise us a life without trouble. Instead he said, *But I am not abandoned. The Father is with me. I've told you all this so that trusting me, you will be unshakable and assured, deeply at peace. In this godless world you will continue to experience difficulties. But take heart! I've conquered the world.* John 16:33 (The Message)

My journal entry from March 20, 2018
Good Morning, Lord.
I slept restlessly last night. This morning I woke feeling tired. I started my day by reading passages from Mark, filled with accounts of miraculous healings.

Our recent Bible study about getting through tough times identified some areas where we still need to heal — stuff we thought we dealt with long ago — places where we still hurt.

When I woke in the middle of the night, my cognizant thought was a prayer for Ginger — for a new direction and a new dream — perhaps a new dream for me as well.

Lord, I confess. I don't know how to pray. It's hard to recognize Your purpose for me. I continue to seek. I continue to ask for miraculous healing. I know You've carried me through so much, and I am so grateful.

I ask for strength to endure — strength to stand. I don't understand so many things.

Help me trust even when I don't understand.

I love you, Lord.

I do not know the answers, but I know the One who does!

Praise be to the God and Father of our
Lord Jesus Christ, the Father of compassion
and the God of all comfort,
who comforts us in all our troubles,
so that we can comfort those in
any trouble with the comfort
we ourselves receive
from God.
2 Cor. 1:3-4
(NIV)

Chapter 18
What Can I Do? How Can I Help?
Caring for Those in Crisis

"How are you?" a well-meaning casual acquaintance asked a recently widowed woman.

The abrupt reply shocked everyone standing in the small group gathered near the coffee pot. "How do you expect me to be? I just buried my husband. I'm overwhelmed and grief-stricken."

Have you ever found yourself in a similar situation? Perhaps, you spoke the right words at the wrong time. In an effort to comfort, something escaped your mouth and you wished for a rewind button. Faced with two options, you either continued to talk making a bad situation worse or exited awkwardly wondering how to fix things.

My experience as a cancer survivor as well as a personal and professional caregiver confirmed people's incredible capacity to provide for emotional and physical needs. However, sometimes we lack discretion. Well-meaning individuals with pure motives may say and do hurtful things.

My own personal experience with well-intentioned comments provided an example of what not to do. At my postoperative visit my surgeon intended to encourage me. "Your incision is well healed. Everything looks great and your pathology confirms DCIS (ductal carcinoma in situ).

When is your appointment with radiation oncology? Since you work in the building, radiation will be like a coffee break for you."

I wanted to reach across the room and slap him. He'd delivered the best possible news. Compared to my friends and the patients for whom I cared, I required minimal follow up treatment and I celebrated an excellent prognosis. However, I left the office that day feeling diminished. I said nothing.

Though very grateful for a good report, the overwhelming response resonated in my mind. "Oh yeah, Buddy, it's certainly not a coffee break I ever wanted to take."

A good friend recently walked through her own journey with a DCIS diagnosis. She recalled how often she had remarked to her patients how fortunate they were to have DCIS as opposed to a more aggressive form of breast cancer. Faced with her own treatment trajectory, she realized how the statement minimized the individual's experience. "Everything changes when faced with the mutilation of your own body. I'll never say it's *just* DCIS again – or *just* anything else for that matter. Cancer is cancer. Each person deserves full support for their journey."

The ideas that follow are a compilation of thoughts from many people who walked through tough times. Some come from those who faced illness, their own and/or the illness of a family member. Others walked through grief from the loss of a spouse or a child.

Each of us gratefully acknowledge the support and love of friends, family and caring strangers. The love and support of others sustained us through unimaginable circumstances.

2 Corinthians 1:3-4 encourages us to comfort each other. *Praise be to the God and Father of our Lord Jesus Christ, the Father of compassion and the God of all comfort, who comforts us in all our troubles, so that we can comfort those in any trouble with the comfort we ourselves receive from God. (NIV)*

As we walk through this life, we all confront struggles. Each person will face difficult situations. We share these thoughts to encourage caring people who want to know how to best support others through crisis.

HELPFUL CONVERSATIONS

- Trust yourself. Gather the best information you can. Make your decisions based on that information. Don't spend time looking back or second-guessing yourself.
- I am here if you need me…to talk, to listen or just to be here.
- I wish I had the right words, just know I care.
- I don't know how you feel, but I am here to help in any way I can.
- I am so sorry (for the loss, or for the situation). *The most comforting thing that really anyone can say is "that sucks and I am so sorry!"*
- I am praying for you – Then DO PRAY – FOLLOW THROUGH.
- Ask, "May I pray for you right now"? Stop right then and pray.
- You can also send notes where you have written out your prayer.

- One friend posted our daughter's name on her refrigerator and prayed for us each time she saw the name. *"God, I don't know the need today, but You do. Please, meet whatever her need is today."*
- I care that you are hurting.
- Say nothing – just give a big hug. This speaks that you care and love.
- Be there – just be there.
- Sit in silence.
- Listen more – talk less.
- Encourage.
- Be sensitive to know how and when sharing your story may be helpful.
- Know when to be silent and keep your stories to yourself.
- Give a hug instead of saying something.
- I am here for you.
    - I'm always a phone call away.
    - I am usually up early (or late) if you need to talk.
- You can ask if it's okay to talk about the loved one.
    - You might want to say, "I will always remember how…."
    - Reminisce with the family about the loved one.
    - It's good to share old photos you might have of yourself and the loved one. The family may have never seen these.
    - My favorite memory of your loved one is…

UNHELPFUL COMMENTS AND ACTIONS

AVOID:
- Preaching – Even great wisdom delivered at the wrong time can be more hurtful than helpful.
- Overstating the obvious.
- Talking about the patient as if they are not in the room.
- Acting as if there is no hope.
- Acting as if the person is dying or already dead.
- Feel you need to fill the air with words.
- Telling a hurting person about your relative or friend who died from the same disease.
- Sharing your "horror stories" of treatment of disease.
- Offering unsolicited advice
- Telling the person how they should feel.
- Giving up hope.
- Expecting God to work on your time table or to act in the way you want.

WHAT NOT TO SAY:
- "I know exactly what you are going through."
    - Even though you may have experienced the death of a loved one, it is impossible to know exactly what someone else is experiencing.
    - Even when experiences mirror each other, the reactions will differ because everyone experiences pain, grief, and loss on their own terms.

- Don't presume to speak for God such as:
  - "God must have needed her more," or "She was such a good person God wanted her to be with Him."
  - "Her days were numbered and her number was up."
  - "There is a reason for everything."
  - "She did what she came here to do and it was her time to go."
  - Remember everyone has their own view of God.
- Another often-repeated painful comment – *He or she is in a better place.* While this may be theologically sound, it is not what a grieving spouse, parent, or child needs to hear at the moment.
- Don't assume to know God's will. *Declaring a tragedy as God's will hurts the individual deeply.*
- At least she (he) lived a long life, many people die young. *Really, how is this comforting?*
- "You can still have another child." or "At least you have other children." or "So, sad, she was their only child." *As if somehow one child replaces another.*
- She/he brought this on herself/himself. *Again, this doesn't comfort, and regardless of the circumstance never appropriate.*
- "It's time to get on with your life." or "Aren't you over him yet, he has been dead for a while now." *Remember – everyone grieves on their own timetable.*
- Never ever start talking about your own experience relating what happened to you.
  - *This is not appropriate.*

- - *Probably the most hurtful expressions were long stories "Well this is what happened to my mother, father or others who suffered with a stroke, or heart attack or other illness."*
  - *"When I was in the hospital dealing with the fears, the staff, the visitors and other issues I did not want to hear others' stories. I wanted them to say that they were there to help me or just listen to me, or just be present with me."*
- People attempt to give advice even when you do not ask for it.
  - *One of the more hurtful things said was "Are you sure you are in the best hospital, have the best doctor, are getting the best care?" It is not a time when you want people to question your choices or your decisions. You don't need anyone causing you to doubt yourself.*
  - *Another young woman added, It is also irritating when they start giving you advice about how they handled something that was usually not even close to what I was experiencing.*
- Just listen and be there.
- Don't minimize the person's experience.
  - *One particularly hurtful comment, "Well, they look just fine and it's hard to imagine anything is wrong." That may be true, but it makes it seem that they think you are exaggerating or making it up.*
  - *Judgment statements don't help — "at least it is the good kind of breast cancer to have." While that may be true, having to mutilate your body for any cancer is still bad.*

- Don't tell someone how they should pray or how they should feel.
- Don't make assumptions because the outcome doesn't match expectations.
- "Be strong" – or just as detrimental – "You are so strong."

A young couple shared experiences during the illness and death of their baby. They hated hearing this statement from well-meaning church friends. *God won't give you more than you can handle. "Really! I will never believe that God is the one who dished out our stuff. It was Satan. Just like in Job, it was not God who did the horrible things, but He did provide, and He did replace all that was lost."*

I share her perspective. It is much better to say you are so sorry for the situation and God is still there. He will provide in ways you might not see or know. We live in a fallen world, and until God redeems the earth, horrible things will happen.

The same couple equally hated hearing comments about their strength. *You're so strong to deal with everything. I don't know how you can stand this.*

Another young mother expressed the similar sentiment. *Least favorite thing people say is "God will never give you more than you can handle." It is so trite and unhelpful. It is very invalidating and frankly, makes me want to punch someone.*

From the perspective of the strugglers who may be barely hanging on: *We certainly don't feel strong – We do what we have to do – there is no other choice. We learn the reality – God's **power is made perfect in our weaknesses.***

It would be far better to say. *I admire you. This must be incredibly difficult. I am here if you need to lean on someone.*

During the time I needed it most, another friend shared a piece of bumper sticker theology. Intended to bring a smile, it worked perfectly. *If God will never give me more than I can handle, I wish He didn't think I was so strong.*

HELPFUL ACTS OF KINDNESS

- Do household chores.
- Hiring a housecleaner once a week. This would work best for a group of people to contribute money, so that it could be done long term. One person would need to coordinate this and not be shy about asking friends for contributions. The coordinator would also be the one to communicate with the housecleaner about the patient's special requests about the house.
- *Cleaning for a Reason* might be a good resource for women with cancer in active treatment.[11]
- Meals – use an online app such as *Meal Train*[12] or *Take Them a Meal*[13] where preferences can be listed for days and times, as well as what types of food the family likes.
- Family can leave two coolers on their porch – one for cold food and one for hot food. The person delivering food can text the family so they know their meal has arrived and is in the cooler. Often the family doesn't have the energy to greet people at the door, but the meal is still appreciated.

---

[11] (http://cleaningforareason.org/)
[12] (https://www.mealtrain.com/)
[13] (https://takethemameal.com/)

- Provide gift cards to favorite restaurants for a special evening out, or to fast food or take out places for busy treatment days.
- Offer to write thank you notes for the meals, gifts that are received. The patient may wish to compose a "sample thank you" and then a friend can write these and put postage on and mail.
- A similar idea – provide printed or computer created thank you notes. The patient or family can personalize with a signature. A friend can address, apply postage and mail.
- Meet a specific need. Acts of kindness large and small will be remembered for years to come.
- Grocery shopping.
- Laundry.
- Mow the lawn.
- Run errands.
- Provide meals that freeze in disposable containers
- Loan funny movies or books for children in the family – or even the entire family.
- Make the days for doctor visits or treatments special by treating the patient to a favorite restaurant or on a patio in nice weather.
- Send cards, texts or e-mails. They can be read and re-read, bringing comfort when the person is alone.
- Encouraging scriptures on cards or post-it notes to place around the house or hospital room. Sometimes it is only one Bible thought at a time that can be absorbed.

- If the patient would like, a friend could come and watch TV with patient. No words need to be said – just the presence of a friend in the room.
- Bring a game to the hospital room for children of the patient to play while spending time with the parent.
- Surprises, such as a check or gift card, tucked into a note are always helpful.
- Be normal. Normalcy is hard, but desperately needed.
- Be yourself.
- Laugh when appropriate. Healing laughter can be safety valve for pent-up emotions.
- Find ways to celebrate the present.
- Allow the patient and family to express their feelings. They may experience the gambit of emotions and may change from moment to moment.
- Babysit. Give the parents time to be alone as a couple.
- Be sensitive to clues that indicate unspoken needs.
- Hope.
- Pray for your friend and with them when appropriate.
- Be consistent.
- Don't say, "Let me know if there's anything I can do." If you see something that needs to be done, do it. Don't ask – just do it!
    - The words of three ladies express how much it meant to have someone see the need and meet it.

I was so thankful when my mom would just do things without asking, because I was so overwhelmed that I could not even verbalize what I needed at times. We kept a whiteboard with a list of several things that could always be done.

On two occasions after great trauma in my life I returned home to find friends at my kitchen sink washing my dishes. Somehow this provided great comfort.

One young woman shared. *Having someone just come and do simple things that I wouldn't think to request proved so helpful. After my surgery, my friend drove me to the salon to have my hair washed. This loving gesture comforted me, lifted my spirits, and made me feel human.*

She continued. *Making time to call, say hello, and talk about anything except the crisis is important, too. You get sick of always talking about your problems.*

Oh, how I identify with her sentiment. I often thought, *If I'm sick of talking about this, everyone else has to be sick of listening.*

Another good friend similarly expressed, *It just gets so old.*

Sometimes we simply need to be normal.

HELPFUL SUPPORT FOR THE CAREGIVER

- Invite the caregiver out to lunch, which provides for continued contact with the outside social world and an opportunity to talk, if that is desired.
- Give a journal to the caregiver to take notes at the doctor visit for the patient. Taking notes at the doctor is NOT the responsibility of the patient.
- Journaling allows the caregiver to express deep emotions in a safe place – fears, doubts, prayers, blessings, insights, memories.
- Provide encouraging scriptures on index cards or post-it notes.

Remember – Once the immediate crisis passes, emotional pain and grief may persist.

"Don't think that you have to do something for the family of a loved one immediately after the death. Often the family remembers and appreciates acts done long after the funeral. One friend ordered a beautiful rose bush for our garden because it reminded them of our daughter. This was done about a year after her passing. Another friend sent us a check in a card on the first anniversary of her death for a tree of our choosing to plant in our yard. These acts were special to us because the friends knew of our love of flowers and trees. Those will be a forever reminder."

"People continued to remember me long after the funeral. They still called, invited me to go to coffee, took me for a drive, or included me in events with their families. They offered to do little things for me. For example, *I am going to the store. Do you need anything?*"

"It helps to be remembered when you feel so alone and sad. The ladies of our community supported me and helped me get back into *life again, not just as an observer or on the sidelines.* They provided comfort from sincere hearts."

Job 28

There is a mine for silver and a place where gold is refined.
Iron is taken from the earth, and copper is smelted from ore.
Mortals put an end to the darkness;
they search out the farthest recesses
for ore in the blackest darkness.
Far from human dwellings they cut a shaft, in places
untouched by human feet;
far from other people they dangle and sway.
The earth, from which food comes,
is transformed below as by fire;
lapis lazuli comes from its rocks,
and its dust contains nuggets of gold.
No bird of prey knows that hidden path,
no falcon's eye has seen it.
Proud beasts do not set foot on it, and no lion prowls there.
People assault the flinty rock with their hands
and lay bare the roots of the mountains.
They tunnel through the rock; their eyes see all its treasures.
They search the sources of the river
and bring hidden things to light.
But where can wisdom be found?
Where does understanding dwell?
No mortal comprehends its worth;
it cannot be found in the land of the living.
The deep says, "It is not in me"
The sea says, "It is not with me."
It cannot be bought with the finest gold,
nor can its price be weighed out in silver.

It cannot be bought with the gold of Ophir,
with precious onyx or lapis lazuli.
Neither gold nor crystal can compare with it,
nor can it be had for jewels of gold.
Coral and jasper are not worthy of mention;
the price of wisdom is beyond rubies.
The topaz of Cush cannot compare with it;
it cannot be bought with pure gold.
Where then does wisdom come from?
Where does understanding dwell?
It is hidden from the eyes of every living thing,
concealed even from the birds in the sky.
Destruction and Death say,
"Only a rumor of it has reached our ears."
God understands the way to it
and he alone knows where it dwells,
for he views the ends of the earth
and sees everything under the heavens.
When he established the force of the wind
and measured out the waters,
when he made a decree for the rain
and a path for the thunderstorm,
then he looked at wisdom and appraised it;
he confirmed it and tested it.
And he said to the human race,
"The fear of the Lord—that is wisdom,
and to shun evil is understanding."
Job 28 (NIV)

Chapter 19
The Refiner's Purpose

The refiner carefully arranges his tools.

He chooses a piece of hardened rock which holds the promise of rare, valuable metal hidden deep inside. Careful inspection of the stone suggests treasured silver. He places the specimen on his workbench.

Grasping a familiar chisel and hammer, he strikes the rock at a perfect angle. It breaks apart, revealing buried metals. The seasoned craftsman looks beyond the marred elements. *It will take a lot of work, but the end result will justify the effort.*

Making careful preparation, the refiner heats the furnace to the precise temperature – hot enough to remove other metals contaminating the quality of the silver – but not so hot as to destroy the desired product. He carefully selects an appropriate container, one designed to withstand the intense heat. Then, he gathers the broken, crushed ore and places it in the vessel. Prepared to oversee the entire process, he positions the crucible into the furnace.

Under the attentive eye of the refiner, the ore melts in the crucible, and a layer of dross rises to the surface. After painstakingly skimming the impurities from the surface, he adds boric acid, turns up the heat, and returns the crucible to the blistering furnace. Experience provides the knowledge that certain impurities are only released at specific temperatures. He brushes aside the dross, which disintegrates into a useless pile of ashes.

Over and over, the silversmith repeats the process. With skill and patience, the refiner removes the dross, leaving behind glistening silver – each time more pure and precious. To measure his progress, he looks for his own reflection on the surface of the silver-filled crucible. Initially, the image bears little resemblance to the creator. After each process, the likeness clears, becoming less distorted.

As the ore stares at the pile of dross, she begins to understand the process. With each emergence from the crucible, she gazes into the face of the refiner. Recognizing additional imperfections, she continues to submit to the fire until she observes the creator's satisfied expression. At last, she reflects the desired image.

Finally, the precious metal attains its highest level of purity. The silver emerges from the furnace, and her shining surface clearly reflects the image of the refiner. The process is complete.

God created us in His image. He desires to reclaim us perfected. He continues to refine us and make us pure and holy, in the image of Christ.

When I emerge from the crucible for the final time and step into the presence of God, He will behold a purified, perfectly molded creation.

My Creator – my Redeemer – my Refiner will see me through my savior's eyes. He will smile and declare, "This is my perfected, beloved child. She is purified and finally all she was created to be."

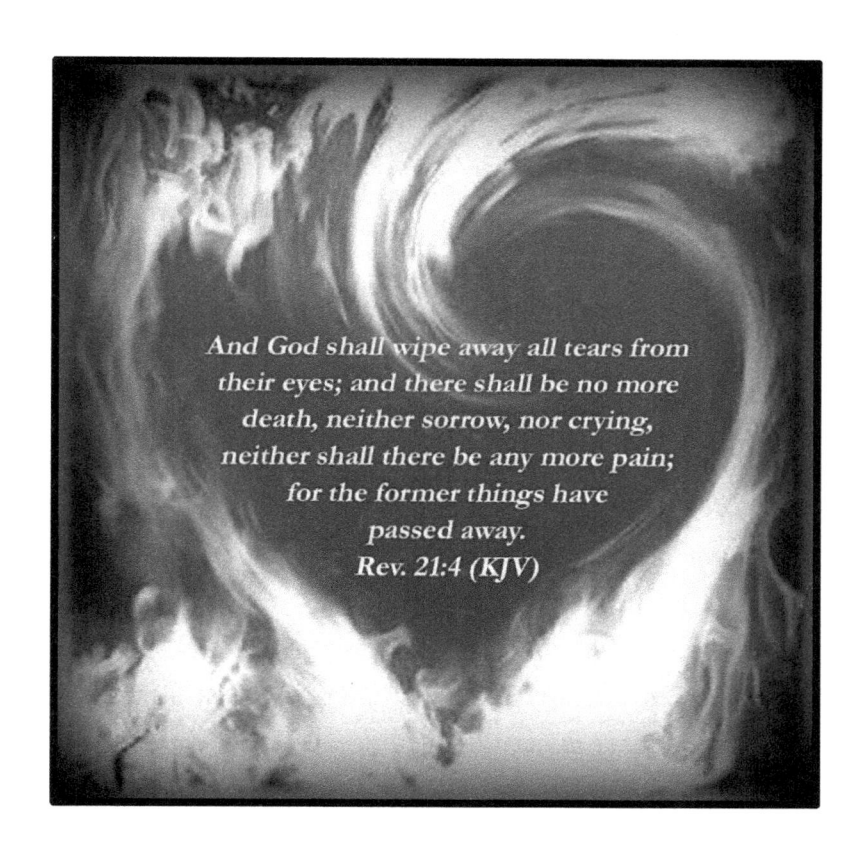

And God shall wipe away all tears from
their eyes; and there shall be no more
death, neither sorrow, nor crying,
neither shall there be any more pain;
for the former things have
passed away.
Rev. 21:4 (KJV)

Chapter 20
Hanging onto Hope
Comforting Scriptures

The LORD is my shepherd; I shall not want.
He maketh me to lie down in green pastures:
he leadeth me beside the still waters.
He restoreth my soul: he leadeth me in the paths of righteousness
for his name's sake.
Yea, though I walk through the valley of the shadow of death,
I will fear no evil: for thou art with me;
thy rod and thy staff they comfort me.
Thou preparest a table before me in the presence of mine enemies:
thou anointest my head with oil; my cup runneth over.
Surely goodness and mercy shall follow me all the days of my life:
and I will dwell in the house of the LORD forever.
Psalm 23 (KJV)

Have not I commanded thee? Be strong and of a good courage; be not afraid, neither be thou dismayed: for the LORD thy God is with thee whithersoever thou goest.
Joshua 1:9 (KJV)

In the same way, the spirit helps us in our weakness. We do not know what we ought to pray for, but the Spirit himself intercedes for us through wordless groans.
Romans 8:26 (NIV)

But they that wait upon the LORD shall renew their strength; they shall mount up with wings as eagles; they shall run, and not be weary; and they shall walk, and not faint.
Isaiah 40:31 (KJV)

*Trust in the L*ORD *with all thine heart;*
and lean not unto thine own understanding.
In all thy ways acknowledge him,
and he shall direct thy paths.
Proverbs 3:5-6 (KJV)

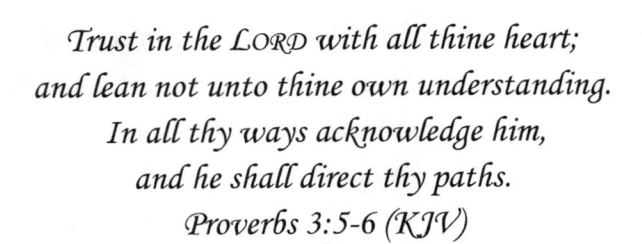

And we know that in all things God works
for the good of those who love him,
who have been called according to his purpose.
Romans 8:28 (NIV)

For I know the plans I have for you,"
*declares the L*ORD*,*
"plans to prosper you and not to harm you,
plans to give you hope and a future.
Then you will call on me and come and pray to me,
and I will listen to you.
You will seek me and find me
when you seek me with all your heart.
Jeremiah 29:11-13 (NIV)

*The LORD will fulfill his purpose for me;
thy steadfast love, O LORD, endures forever.
Do not forsake the work of thy hands.
Psalm 138: 8 (RSV)*

*Rejoice in the Lord always.
I will say it again: Rejoice!
Let your gentleness be evident to all.
The Lord is near.
Do not be anxious about anything,
but in every situation, by prayer and petition,
with thanksgiving, present your requests to God.
And the peace of God, which transcends all understanding, will
guard your hearts and your minds in Christ Jesus.
Philippians 4: 4-7 (NIV)*

*I can do all things through Christ which strengtheneth me.
Philippians 4:13 (KJV)*

Celebrate God all day, every day. I mean, revel in him!
Make it as clear as you can to all you meet
that you're on their side,
working with them and not against them.
Help them see that the Master is about to arrive.
He could show up any minute!
Don't fret or worry. Instead of worrying, pray.
Let petitions and praises shape your worries into prayers, letting God know your concerns.
Before you know it, a sense of God's wholeness, everything coming together for good,
will come and settle you down.
It's wonderful what happens when Christ displaces worry at the center of your life…
Whatever I have, wherever I am,
I can make it through anything
in the One who makes me who I am.
Philippians 4:4-7, 13
(The Message)

You, God, are my God, earnestly I seek you;
I thirst for you, my whole being longs for you,
in a dry and parched land where there is no water.
I have seen you in the sanctuary
and beheld your power and your glory.
Because your love is better than life,
my lips will glorify you.
I will praise you as long as I live, and in your name.
I will lift up my hands.
I will be fully satisfied as with the richest of foods;
with singing lips my mouth will praise you.
On my bed I remember you;
I think of you through the watches of the night.
Because you are my help,
I sing in the shadow of your wings.
I cling to you; your right hand upholds me.
Those who want to kill me will be destroyed;
they will go down to the depths of the earth.
They will be given over to the sword
and become food for jackals.
But the king will rejoice in God;
all who swear by God will glory in him,
while the mouths of liars will be silenced.
Psalm 63
(NIV)

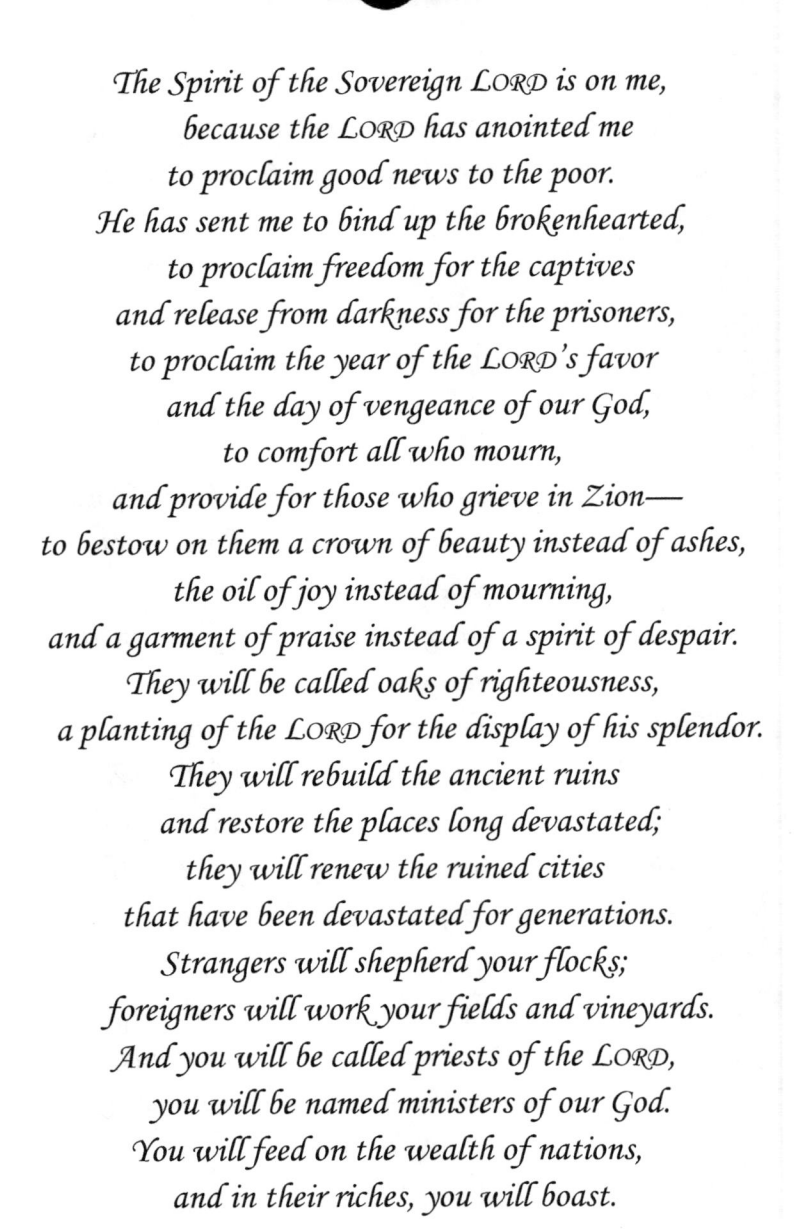

The Spirit of the Sovereign LORD *is on me,*
because the LORD *has anointed me*
to proclaim good news to the poor.
He has sent me to bind up the brokenhearted,
to proclaim freedom for the captives
and release from darkness for the prisoners,
to proclaim the year of the LORD*'s favor*
and the day of vengeance of our God,
to comfort all who mourn,
and provide for those who grieve in Zion—
to bestow on them a crown of beauty instead of ashes,
the oil of joy instead of mourning,
and a garment of praise instead of a spirit of despair.
They will be called oaks of righteousness,
a planting of the LORD *for the display of his splendor.*
They will rebuild the ancient ruins
and restore the places long devastated;
they will renew the ruined cities
that have been devastated for generations.
Strangers will shepherd your flocks;
foreigners will work your fields and vineyards.
And you will be called priests of the LORD*,*
you will be named ministers of our God.
You will feed on the wealth of nations,
and in their riches, you will boast.

Instead of your shame
you will receive a double portion,
and instead of disgrace,
you will rejoice in your inheritance.
And so you will inherit a double portion in your land,
and everlasting joy will be yours.
"For I, the LORD, love justice;
I hate robbery and wrongdoing.
In my faithfulness I will reward my people
and make an everlasting covenant with them.
Their descendants will be known among the nations
and their offspring among the peoples.
All who see them will acknowledge
that they are a people the LORD has blessed."
I delight greatly in the LORD;
my soul rejoices in my God.
For he has clothed me with garments of salvation
and arrayed me in a robe of his righteousness,
as a bridegroom adorns his head like a priest,
and as a bride adorns herself with her jewels.
For as the soil makes the sprout come up
and a garden causes seeds to grow,
so the Sovereign LORD will make righteousness
and praise spring up before all nations.
Isaiah 61 (NIV)

*Rejoice always,
Pray continually,
Give thanks in all circumstances;
for this is God's will for you in Christ Jesus.
Do not quench the Spirit.
Do not treat prophecies with contempt
but test them all;
Hold on to what is good,
reject every kind of evil.
May God himself, the God of peace,
sanctify you through and through.
May your whole spirit,
soul and body be kept blameless
at the coming of our Lord Jesus Christ.
The one who calls you is faithful,
and he will do it.
1 Thessalonians 5:16-24 (NIV)*

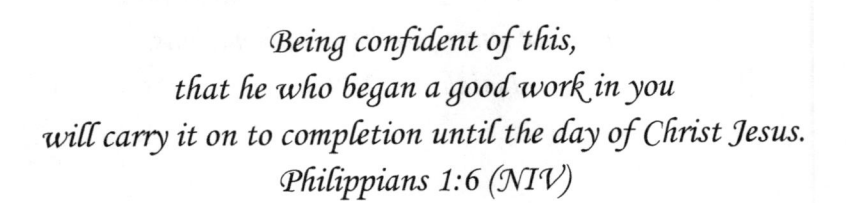

*Being confident of this,
that he who began a good work in you
will carry it on to completion until the day of Christ Jesus.
Philippians 1:6 (NIV)*

References

(Claypool, J. (1974). *Tracks of a Fellow Struggler; Living and Growing Through Grief.* New Orleans: Insight Press.

Harling, R. (1987). *Steel Magnolias.* New York: Wharton and Garrison, LLP.

http://cleaningforareason.org/. (n.d.)

https://returntonow.net/2017/09/22/85-people-hate-jobs-gallup-poll-says/. (n.d.).

https //takethemameal.com/. (n.d.).

https://www.cancer.org/involved/fundraise/relay-for-life.html. (n.d.).

https://www.mealtrain.com/. (n.d.).

HTTPS://WWW.SAMARITANSPURSE.ORG/OUR-MINISTRY/ABOUT-US/. (n.d.).

https://www.stjude.org/disease/medulloblastoma.html. (n.d.).

https://www.stjude.org/disease/medulloblastoma.html. (n.d.).

https://www.stjude.org/disease/medulloblastoma.html. (n.d.).

https://www.stjude.org/disease/medulloblastoma.html. (n.d.).

https://www.stjude.org/disease/medulloblastoma.html. (n.d.).

Lucado, M. (2013). *You'll Get Through This.* Nashville, TN: Thomas Nelson Publishers.

Majors, K. D. (2017). *Daring to Hope.* Colorado Springs: Multnomah.

www.collinsdictionary.com. (n.d.).

ABOUT THE AUTHOR

A native Texan, Wanda Strange resides with her husband, Kerry, in Bluff Dale, Texas. Married since 1969, they are the parents of an adult daughter, Ginger.

She loves music, movies, books, and passionately pursues time with family and friends. Steadfast faith and a renewed sense of her Maker's purpose for her life provides motivation to share the stories of God's faithfulness through difficult circumstances.

Though Wanda retired in 2016, her love of oncology nursing fuels a desire to serve her family, friends, and community. The passion for patients and caregivers inspires her to encourage cancer patients, their families, and oncology colleagues.

Committed to the concept of purposeful living, she desires to make a difference throughout her life.

Faith – family – friends comprise the priorities of Wanda's busy life.

CPSIA information can be obtained
at www.ICGtesting.com
Printed in the USA
LVHW082333050721
691944LV00021B/770

9 781732 536302